THE WINNER IN ME

First published in 1999 by
Marino Books
an imprint of Mercier Press
16 Hume Street Dublin 2
Tel: (01) 661 5299; Fax: (01) 661 8583
E.mail: books@marino.ie

Trade enquiries to CMD Distribution
55A Spruce Avenue
Stillorgan Industrial Park
Blackrock County Dublin
Tel: (01) 294 2556; Fax: (01) 294 2564
E.mail: cmd@columba.ie

ISBN 1 86023 102 0
10 9 8 7 6 5 4 3 2 1

A CIP record for this title is available
from the British Library

Cover photo courtesy of Pat Baker
Cover design by SPACE

Printed by Cox & Wyman Ltd,
Reading, Berks UK

THE WINNER IN ME

DON BAKER'S STORY

JACKIE HAYDEN

CONTENTS

1

Been Down So Long

I could imagine them all talking about me. There's that Don Baker fella. Saw him on the telly. Thinks he's it, playing that harmonica and singing the blues. Well he's got the blues now, that's for sure. Look at him now, barely able to stand up. Disgraceful, throwing up in the street like that. Has he no shame?

Yes, I'd been physically sick many times before but this time it was different. It was half past eight in the morning and I was stumbling down a road in Ballybough, a busy suburb on the northside of Dublin. People scurried by on their way to work, trying to wake up, while I hadn't yet been to bed. Housewives busied themselves with groceries and kids passed by on their way to school while I, at thirty-three years of age, was occupied in trying to hide my embarrassment and my shame as I puked up my guts all over the public pathway.

Were they talking about me? Were those kids laughing at me, sniggering behind their hands? Or worse, were they pitying me? Some of them might even be fans, the very people who paid my wages. How little they knew about where their money went as soon as I got my hands on it and the havoc it was wreaking on my life.

Yes, it was the drink again. It had become an increasingly worrisome burden in my life over many years, but there was now another potential catastrophe besetting my life, one that was – quite literally, in the circumstances – the only factor likely to have a sobering effect on me. Jo, my wife of a mere two years, was threatening to leave me unless I quit drinking for good. She'd had enough of my loutish behaviour and could clearly see what I refused to see, that my drunken habits were in danger of spoiling what had begun as a happy marriage. What was even worse, she felt my behaviour was threatening the welfare of my pride and joy, our baby daughter Jordana. Jo was going to leave me.

But if Jo left me now I would almost certainly also lose our Jordana, an innocent of five months to whom I was now doing exactly what my own father had done to me nearly three decades ago. Do we never learn?

Of course I had promised Jo countless times that I was going to stop, but there was always an excuse for one more drink, one more night out, one more session with the lads, one more woman to impress with my macho bravado. But something inside me convinced me that she had finally reached the end of her patience this time and there would be no turning back once she left.

But God knows I'd tried often enough, really tried.

I'd give up for a few days. A week. A month. I'd break out in rashes and then I'd find another bottle. I'd even gone to a doctor in St Dympna's Hospital. I'd tried every pill and tablet on the market, but that too led me nowhere except back to another bottle. I'd been told many times, by friends, colleagues and professionals alike, that there was no hope for me unless I did something serious about it and stopped drinking once and for all. In my alcoholic haze I fully intended to 'do something serious about it', but not just yet. This was a problem I was always planning to sort out tomorrow or next week or, more likely, never.

But if I wasn't yet ready to face the reality and sort myself out once and for all then Jo was, and this time she'd gone as far as to move herself and Jordana out of the flat we shared in Ballybough, which we'd moved into after my mother died. She'd finally blown the whistle. I knew the game was over and I was now into extra time, if it wasn't already too late.

At that time I was a member of a well-respected Dublin rock band called The Business. We had a fairly full diary of gigs, but whatever few pounds I earned I drank. I borrowed money from friends. I even drank Jo's money to the extent that I'd cleaned out her entire bank savings account. This was hardly encouraging behaviour towards a comparatively new wife and certainly no responsible way to bring up a baby.

Despite my life as a musician and the growing trade of hard drugs in Dublin, I was a real Irish traditionalist.

Drugs other than alcohol never tempted me. I never even took to smoking hash because the couple of times I tried it it gave me heartburn. Instead I stuck steadfastly to the one drug that had ruined my father and countless other fathers before him: drink. Beer. Spirits. Brandy and port. Anything, really. I wasn't overly fussy.

It took me a long time, while later attending the treatment centre for alcoholics in Stanhope Street, to learn that it's not the quantity of alcohol you drink. Quite conceivably, someone can drink a bottle of whiskey every night without actually being an alcoholic. Some people find that hard to understand. An alcoholic is not somebody who drinks a lot per se but someone whose drinking causes problems for him in one of the main areas of his life, whether spiritual, physical, mental, social, sexual or emotional. In my own case it had affected every area of my life and was now obviously affecting the well-being of my loved ones as well.

Little did I know at the time but I had been using drink to bury my emotions and to hide from deep-seated fears which could be traced back to traumas I had suffered as a young boy in a deprived working-class family on Dublin's hard-pressed northside.

I managed to get by as a musician, my only source of income, by staying just barely on the right side of being functional, but not always. There were times when I'd let myself and the rest of the band down dreadfully. After a gig in Sheriff Street in the centre of Dublin I ended up hovering dangerously close to the edge of the roof of the venue, twisted drunk. One of my colleagues, Tommy Moore, went green in the face with fright and an Italian guy called Elpedio Salveta saved me from falling to my certain death. But not even that close call with death shook me out of my stupor.

Of course people had been telling me for years that if I didn't stop I'd kill myself, but I'd laughed every one of them off. But now, as I hid my face and my shame from the passers-by on Ballybough Road, I realised that alcohol, which in some ways had had a medicinal effect on me in that it had helped me deal with my emotions and fears, had become a problem that was much bigger than me and far greater than the problems I was using it to hide from myself.

At long last I'd hit the rock bottom I'd been warned about and had been expecting, and secretly hoping for, and which deep down in my soul I knew was inevitable. It was necessary for me to reach that point myself and realise that there were no further depths to which I could sink.

Only when you reach the bottom of that pit can you start to work yourself back up to some sort of normal living pattern. I could sense my own shame and, perhaps worse, I could imagine the pity of the passers-by and their private laughter at my sorry state. Did I have the courage to wake up and take the first step: to stop hiding from the pain that had been tearing me asunder deep inside since childhood? Could I take the necessary actions to save my marriage and the company of my daughter?

It was time to face the truth for the first time in my life: I was a loser. Now it was time, if it was not already too late, to discover if there might be a winner in me too. Little did I know then, but it was going to be a long and painful path.

2

BORN WITH THE BLUES

The pain that lead me down that dark path began when I was almost six years of age and I'm still struggling to come to terms with it today, despite years of counselling sessions, endless hours of therapy, dozens of books, seminars, courses and visits to a variety of rehabilitation centres.

As far as I can trace it back, the seeds of my anxiety first took root when I was taken into Blanchardstown Hospital, on the outer suburbs of Dublin, having been diagnosed as suffering from primary tuberculosis. Unfortunately, the practice of the 1950s was for parents not to be allowed to stay with their young children at the hospital, and that was the kernel of my problem.

Looking back from more than forty years later I can still chillingly remember the feelings of loneliness, abandonment and isolation as if it were today. Even the nurses seemed to me to be very impersonal and quite detached. This was obviously quite natural for them under the circumstances, as they would have had a heavy workload, but it made the wrong impression on me at my tender age.

On arrival I was placed in a room on my own, in a strange world far away from the familiarity of home. Apart from feeding times and visits from nurses to give me thrice-daily jabs in the arse, I hardly saw anybody else all day. I ached with a painful longing for my mother, who came to see me for only about an hour every Wednesday, which was about standard for hospital visits in those days before they became more relaxed about visitors. I wasn't allowed out of my bed, except to visit the toilet directly across the corridor, so contact with other parts of the hospital was also very restricted.

My only other distraction was listening to the radio on a set of headphones provided by the hospital, so I fretted and sobbed all day and night, alone in what felt like a cold and unloving environment, worrying about how things were at home, but most of all missing my mother. Every night I cried myself to sleep in a state of fear and unrelenting anxiety. Any time I asked if I might be allowed to get in touch with my mother the hospital staff would dismiss my forlorn request with a reminder that she'd be up to see me the following Wednesday. Wednesday always seemed an eternity away.

Then when she came she'd ask me to promise that I would be a big, strong boy and not cry when she left, but no matter how hard I tried I'd be distraught when I saw her walking away down the corridor. I could not stop myself rushing out to take just one last look at her departing figure. Then I'd call her name and rush to her and cling to her skirt in the sheer panic and fear of being left alone again. The nurses would prise my little fingers away from her and drag me screaming back to my bed and back to the pain of this strange place.

Sometimes after her departure I'd rush into the toilet and my feeble voice would shout her name in anguish from the window, from where I could see her walking up the avenue that led through the hospital grounds, but she'd ignore my calls of distress even if she heard them.

To add to my sense of being forgotten and abandoned, my father didn't bother to visit me even once during my entire three months' stay in the hospital. The only comfort I had was when a nurse in the hospital befriended me. She could see my suffering and gave me some mothering, tucking me in gently at night and giving me a goodnight kiss. That was sometimes enough to help me get a night's sleep.

But even that relief was not destined to last: she came to me one evening to tell me she was leaving the hospital to get married. I was so shocked by this latest act of abandonment that, in modern psychological parlance, I'm told I took on a false persona from that point on, putting my real self 'on ice', as it were, closing myself down and blocking out all my emotions. Some of those emotions remain unblocked to this day.

Even now I have difficulty sleeping whenever those feelings of loneliness come back to me. Mentally I was later able to rationalise why this turmoil was happening inside me but I don't think I've ever been able to deal with it properly on an emotional level. I've lived with this feeling of abandonment and rejection by women ever since and I carry a permanent irrational fear of being abandoned and rejected by those closest to me, especially any woman with whom I have a serious relationship. The only way I could cope with it then was to block it out of my mind completely, and some may even argue that I'm still deliberately doing exactly that to some degree.

Much to my dismay, I was sent back to that same hospital again when I was about ten years old. Whereas on my first painful visit I had been in a boys' unit which was separated by a corridor from the girls' unit, on my second stay I found that they had reversed the units, so that now I would occupy a room in what had been the girls' unit.

Despite being alone again, and bearing in mind that I was a little older, my fretting was only about a quarter of what it had been on the previous visit, if such distress can be quantified in that way. That deep apprehension was later to resurface, however, and regularly play havoc in my relationships, especially those with women and authority figures. But if I thought that the slightly lessened sense of loneliness on my second visit, compared to the horror of the first, signalled progress, my subsequent life would give the lie to that.

3

CHILDHOOD BLUES

I was born on 26 August 1950. Our first home had been a Corporation-owned house in my Granny's name at 1 Glenchest Road in Whitehall, a working-class suburb on Dublin's northside. When I was about seven we moved a short distance across the main Swords Road to 17 Glenane Road, Larkhill, where we stayed until I was about twelve. Both houses were fine houses, solid-looking to this day, with a parlour, a kitchen, three bedrooms, toilets and so on, and they were owned by Dublin Corporation, to whom we had to pay rent.

By the time of the move to Larkhill there were four of us in the family: my parents and my brother Pat, who born in 1952, two years after me. My three sisters, Catherine (born 1955), Breda (1957) and Ada (1969), had not yet arrived.

My father, Gerard, originally came from a comparatively prosperous family that owned a Georgian house in Frederick Street. He was of medium build, a bit like myself in appearance, and he played the piano as a hobby, although never professionally. He was also very fond of snooker, drinking and cigarettes. He was a regular customer at the Cosmo snooker club in O'Connell Street and was known for his habit of falling asleep under snooker tables from a combination of drink and tiredness. He would often go straight to work from the snooker hall!

My mother was originally Sarah Waldron from Henrietta Street and she had two miscarriages from natural causes before I was born. She was a very glamorous woman of medium height. Her main source of pleasure in life seemed to be men, and she had no difficulty attracting them. She had learned how to look well in inexpensive clothes and always looked after her appearance. I think she was probably a very self-centred woman, although that might have been forced on her by my father's waywardness.

Before my parents got married, my father's own mother came to my mother and pleaded with her not to marry her son Gerard, a sure sign that his reputation for drinking had reached a worrying level even then. Before she met my father my mother had been going out with a doctor, who had asked her to marry him. But the family story was that she didn't feel good enough for him, partly because she felt a little embarrassed by her inadequate literacy skills, so she turned him down.

This was a Dublin before the era of satellite dishes, microwave cookers, foreign holidays, washing machines and two-car families. A television set, if you could afford one at all, was about the height of a family's materialistic ambitions, and as I grew up, the Whitehall area slowly became dotted with television aerials as more and more families acquired a set, often to the envy of their immediate and less-fortunate neighbours.

Those who had jobs more than likely had a five-and-a-half-day week, and there was little in the way of social entertainment other than football matches, the local cinema and the pub, which was then, and still is, if to a lesser extent, the focal point of social life in Dublin outside the home. That inevitably brings with it the potential risk of the curse of alcoholism, a curse that was to hit our family as badly as any other family we knew.

Even as a young child I became acutely aware that my father had become, not to overstate the case, a raving alcoholic, even if the terminology would have meant nothing to me then. There was virtually no public discussion about alcoholism in Ireland at that time anyway, and the term 'alcoholic', if used at all, was less a description of a health problem and more a term of abuse.

But the problems caused by my father's behaviour and that first hospital visit were compounded not much later when I discovered my mother was having an affair with another man.

There was unpleasantness in our house nearly all the time, with constant fighting, ugly screaming matches and name-calling. I'm not going to condemn either of my parents for that. I know now that they had their own individual demons to battle, but at the time it had a bewildering effect on one so young.

My father worked as a waiter in the Gresham Hotel, then regarded as Ireland's poshest establishment, attracting a clientele at the opposite end of the social spectrum from that of the Baker family in Larkhill. He would regularly bring home from his workplace what he called 'trophies', including knives, forks, spoons, and, on one occasion, a very heavy silver sugar bowl that was eventually to be used for a purpose for which it was not intended and which caused me considerable pain and grief, as we shall see.

As you would expect, fights broke out regularly on account of his drinking too much or her having a lover, or whatever; these fights often began over trivial domestic issues. It was like watching a tennis match as my father and mother batted the insults back and forth to one another. 'You've a lover.' 'I haven't got a lover.' 'You're a whore.' 'You're a drunken bastard.' 'You're a prostitute.' 'You're a bad-minded cunt.' You're this, that, the other, non-stop, as the atmosphere became heavier and more threatening. We kids could see his temper rising and would know that the inevitable explosion wasn't far away. He'd reach for a pan or a pot and smack her on the head with it, or give her a dig in the face, all while we looked on helplessly with horror and fear.

One time he reached for his 'trophy' sugar bowl, a hefty weapon to use on anybody. Seeing his intent, I ran between them to prevent him hitting her with it. Fortunately for her, but less so for me, I took the deflected blow on the top of my head. If that bowl had connected with full force on my mother's head it would have smashed her skull and probably killed her. I still carry the scars on my head as a souvenir of that particularly nasty incident.

Windows and furniture got smashed in these rows and the police were often called, but my parents were never charged with any offence, only cautioned as to their future behaviour. After each police visit matters would calm down for a while, then flare up later as tempers again moved towards boiling point.

Despite my father's hurled abuse, my mother was certainly never a prostitute. I've always believed she was quite a flirtatious and sexually attractive woman, with a voluptuous Marilyn Monroe figure, and she was never without a man, either before or after my father died. But I was to discover that she had taken up with a lover in a most disquieting way that still haunts me. One day I accidentally heard her talking to her lover from a public telephone box. Although I was only about ten years old I could understand that she was inviting him to call round to our house after my father had gone out and that she'd leave the door open for him. I could sense this was a wrong thing for her to be doing, and I was devastated enough to start thinking that all the things my father said about her just might be true after all, and again I would suffer the agonising fear of abandonment and the threat of being rejected, just like I had experienced in the hospital.

Even today I can feel an awful anxiety creeping back into my stomach whenever I recall that incident. The revelation really rocked me, but, sadly, my mother didn't seem at all concerned about how I felt, nor about me having rumbled her little secret, and that made me feel even worse. She didn't try to offer any excuse and seemed far more worried that I should tell my dad, so she gave me some cigarettes as a bribe to keep my mouth shut.

Despite the ongoing physical threats and the regular violent incidents in our household, there was never a hint of sexual abuse in the family, although I know there were some sexually abused children in our predominantly Catholic neighbourhood. But while we had several visits from the police about problems in the household, the local priests never came near us. It was a far different scenario from today, where an area of such poverty and deprivation would have a number of active social workers and caring organisations offering practical support, information and advice to those in need. In those days there was nobody you could turn to. Neighbours might suspect, or even know, that there were some serious problems in a particular family, but interfering in another family's internal troubles was not part of the culture of working-class Dublin of that era.

Drinking to excess, even when it led to vicious fighting and damage to people and property, was such a socially acceptable habit that virtually nobody saw much wrong in it at all, and to some extent being able to hold your drink was the first sign that you had achieved manhood. Yet I think I always suspected that the situation in our house reached a level that was considerably worse than the norm for the rest of the area. If I visited other houses I would instinctively feel a warmth or something intangible there that was missing from my own home, even if I was never quite sure precisely what the difference was. Certainly, Christmas in our house was a forlorn time compared to the jollity and celebration of our neighbours.

For example, one Christmas Day when I was about eleven I woke up and realised that both our parents were missing. I'd no idea where they were, but I quickly spotted that there were no toys for any of us kids, including my sister Breda, who was only about three at the time. I was so disturbed that I locked the front door to prevent her going out and seeing all the new bikes, the colourful clothes and the exciting toys the neighbourhood kids had received from Santa Claus. I peeped out at the other kids through the curtains, feeling thoroughly ashamed of our family, left with nothing on what for most Irish children is the happiest day of the year.

Another Christmas my sister Catherine and I took a small hatchet and a knife to a nearby field beside what used to be called the Crofton Airport Hotel (now the Regency) to cut holly and ivy to sell door-to-door so that we could buy a chicken for Christmas as a family treat.

One of my earliest memories of deprivation prompted me to steal some rhubarb from a neighbour's garden. Hardly a hanging offence, but whereas some kids steal apples for the laugh, this was to put some food on our otherwise-empty table.

I also remember an occasion when, obviously having decided that we were in danger of starving unless drastic action was taken, I crept into a neighbour's garden and arrived back in our kitchen a few minutes later holding up a live rabbit by the ears and telling my mother, 'Here, cook this for us!' It seems funny now, but at the time it was an act of sheer survival. (She made me put the rabbit back.)

There was another incident which may have offered a foretaste of my later penchant for violent behaviour, or it might just have been the John Wayne coming out in me. It was even funnier than the theft of the live rabbit, if somewhat cruel. I had saved up for a long time to buy a pellet gun from a bloke who was in his late teens. One day I took the gun upstairs, and when a young neighbour went by on his bike I leaned out our window and shot him in the arse. What with the fright, and the sudden pain, I suppose, he fell against a steel barrier placed on the path opposite our house to protect kids crossing to the school.

Not surprisingly, he was hurt quite badly. I thought this was hilariously funny, until I discovered that a woman had observed everything from her own upstairs window just a few doors down from us. She came rushing across to tell my mother what I'd done and as a result the gun was taken from me and smashed to smithereens. With that, my short-lived career as the northside's answer to John Wayne was over for the moment, and I'm not sure if I ever recovered from that setback!

Apart from such moments of light relief there were very few times of real joy in my life, although I enjoyed going to the pictures at the Grand Cinema in Whitehall as often as I could afford the price of admission. Like most of the kids in our neighbourhood I used to smoke cigarettes in the toilets if I thought I could get away with it. But Harry, the cinema's usher, would threaten to put me outside if he caught me smoking, unless I fulfilled his one condition – I had to sing a song for him. Don't ask me to explain why. I'm told I had a good, high-pitched voice, and my usual repertoire was a song I loved by Joe Brown about a yellow dress. In fact, I suppose I could regard those enforced perform-ances as the first public singing engagements of my career, and the fact that they took place in a public toilet probably served as a useful preparation for some of the God-awful places I played in later as a profes-sional musician. The fee, too, was almost as paltry!

Like most of my schoolmates I used to like reading comics like the *Beezer*. My favourite character was Roadrunner, and my mouth would water as I read about him devouring an endless supply of chickens, which to us would have been a treat of heavenly proportions. I'm not overstating the case when I say that there were many times when we did not know when, or even if, we might eat again. We were hungry for much of the time, but it was something we tried to keep to ourselves as much as possible, for the sake of pride.

Back then I felt ashamed because we had to put coats on our beds to keep us warm at night, although, as I later learned, this was a common practice in Dublin households. I don't think even our nearest relations were aware of our real plight, but if they were they certainly did nothing to help us.

Occasionally our problems would be alleviated by contributions from the St Vincent de Paul charity organisation, which would supply us with vouchers that we could then trade in for food, clothes or other items we needed. Whenever they called, my mother would send us all upstairs, although I was never sure why she did this.

A kindly neighbour called Mrs Byrne, who worked in the local school, was always very concerned about my mother's welfare. At the end of the school day she'd collect any sandwiches left over by the schoolkids and bring them around to our house for our dinner. I used to hate Fridays because this was the era when Catholics still observed the Friday ban on meat and all the sandwiches for that day would be cheese or jam, but definitely no meat. If the meat was brawn, which I didn't like, I'd throw it away and just eat the bread. How ironic that my father had a good job serving the best food in the poshest hotel in Ireland and we had to rely on other people's scraps for our dinner. Mrs Byrne died quite recently and I felt bad when I heard the news of her passing, since I had never bothered to take the time to thank that woman properly for her thoughtfulness and her kindness to a family who badly needed help in their struggle for survival.

4

GAMES AND EGG-COLLECTING

Ours was not a great house for pets at the best of times, but when I was about five we had a dog called Teddy. That was in the days when horse-drawn carts were still commonplace around the streets of Dublin and the suburbs, and probably throughout the country too. They were used for delivering all sorts of stuff door-to-door, from coal, logs and turf to fruit and vegetables, and they were usually fully equipped with a weighing scales to weigh out the required amount of goods. Unfortunately one of these carts ran over Teddy and killed him, totally devastating me, as losing a pet would devastate any kid of that age.

We probably had other dogs around the house from time to time, but Teddy is the only one I recall with any clarity. I can remember making a mix of bread and milk for him in the days of such doggy delicacies as Pedigree Chum or PAL-Prolongs Active Life! But then our household was not always the safest place for pets.

One day my mother arrived back in the house to find myself and my brother Pat with a cat up on the kitchen table. I was armed with a large hatchet and our plan was to kill the cat so we could use the back part to make one of those coonskin hats with the tail attached which we'd seen being worn by Davy Crockett and other heroes of the Wild West. Fortunately for the cat my mother's sudden arrival, complete with her demand to know 'What in the name of Jaysus are you pair up to now?' put a swift end to our argument as to which of us was to get the rear end of the cat – and spared one of its lives. I'm sure it needed all nine and then some.

But this was all part of the innocence of childhood. We would have seen magical drawings of figures like Davy Crockett in the various comics that I used to collect so avidly, and they painted a picture of a world we'd have loved to escape to, had it ever existed, a fact we never paused to doubt for a second.

Another incident from those days was to have an unexpected and surprisingly positive affect on my harmonica-playing in my professional life. Those who have heard me in my later musical career will probably be familiar with a instrumental harmonica piece I perform called 'Don's Train'. It's a very fast piece, with some tricky sections. I've had some of the top harmonica players in the world, like The Adlers from Israel, ask me how I do some of the things I do in that tune. To be honest, I could not understand why guys' at their level should have so much difficulty with the piece, and I'm not being falsely modest.

Then one day, while brushing my teeth, I suddenly

remembered that there's a piece missing from the tip of my tongue. That missing piece is the perfect size to enable the tip of my tongue to fit right into one of the holes in the harmonica, and that was the explanation for my supposed wizardry on that tune.

With that realisation I also recalled how I had fortunately, as it now turned out, lost that piece from my tongue. One day, while I was still a kid, I was helping my mother lift a pram with one of the other kids in it up a step, and in the process the pram moved forward more easily than expected and a part of it nicked a bit of my tongue off. When I was taken to the hospital they put a ring in it instead of stitches. For that week the only food I could take was soup I sucked through a straw.

So next time Danny Adler or one of the other guys asks me how I play that piece I'll have to tell them that they can all do it. All they have to do is cut a bit off their tongue! Then again, maybe I shouldn't so easily admit that such a thought-provoking part of my technique has such a mundane explanation.

Of course this story has a somewhat serious side to it as well, in that it showed me that even such a negative and traumatic childhood incident could in later life have an unforeseen benefit. It seems to be part of a pattern with me that some of the negative things in my early life are mirrored later on, except more positively, like my being in prison and then performing the role of a prisoner in *In the Name of the Father*, to cite another example.

While I later became a teacher of sorts through my harmonica tutor books and video, I can only recall one teacher from my own early days, and that was Mr Clandillon. I think of him as a fairly decent sort, a dapper, very fair and gentle man most of the time, although he could hand out the punishment when he wanted to, just like the others. I suspected he had a soft spot for me, though.

Perhaps it's strange, but I can't remember much of any of the other teachers or any of my schoolmates. Corporal punishment was accepted at that time and I recall a chap called Moloney getting a very bad beating from one of the teachers. If you were late for school in the morning you almost automatically got the six 'biffs' on the hand, a particularly unpleasant experience on a cold morning, when you'd have to blow on your fingers afterwards to ease the stinging.

But I may have blocked out a lot of my own experiences because in those days you were taught to fear your teachers. If a kid got into trouble with a teacher at school he was just as likely to get a second beating at home. Whereas today a parent might actually go down to a school to sort out a teacher if it was thought he'd overstepped the mark, in my schooldays teachers ruled unquestioned and unchallenged, no matter what they did.

Apart from the days I spent mitching, riding horses and once even getting badly kicked by a horse, in a lot of my spare time outside school hours I played around in the nearby Santry woods. I'd go home from school, put on my wellington boots, put a knife down the boots to convince myself I was going trapping in the outback and head off in search of adventure and freedom, leaving my troubles at home.

I'd pick bunches of bulrushes and when it got dark I'd dip their spongy tops one by one into petrol, light them and enjoy watching them slowly burn. It was easy to get petrol then, as few cars would have had locks on their petrol tanks.

An ash tree beside a river presented us with a challenge: to see who could reach the top, from where you would get a panoramic view over the whole wood. We'd also use lengths of rope to swing from tall branches. Bits of branches would be converted to make bows and arrows. We'd peel off the bark and stick a bird's feather in the tail for extra effect. By using a kind of chicken wire to strengthen the ends and catgut from a fishing rod, we could fire an arrow a considerable distance even with such crude materials. They could certainly be dangerous if they were not handled properly.

This was a time long before the affluence which made the sophisticated toys of today very commonplace. Back then we had to create our own toys and our own games, and the wood provided us with plenty of opportunities and many of the raw materials we needed for them.

A piece of rope would do for skipping. A hurling stick or a lump of wood and a ball would do for a game of rounders, which is a little like baseball. Marbles was another popular game, as you vied to win as many marbles from your mates as you could. Conkers, played by putting a string through chestnuts and taking turns to attempt to break the other person's conker, was hugely popular every autumn, as we scoured the fields and woods in search of chestnuts fallen from the trees. Some of the serious competitors would try any trick to make their chestnut harder: heating it over a fire while making sure it didn't crack was one useful method. It seems to be one of the few such games to survive down the years, and I've even seen my own son at it.

'Relievio' was a robust chasing game which usually involved one team trying to catch all the members of the other team. When one person was captured he was put into an area which served as a kind of jail, but if an uncaptured member of his team could get into the 'jail' and shout 'Relievio!' then the people in the jail would be free to escape. (It's odd how often prisons have featured in my life, even since early childhood!)

I was also a keen egg-collector, although I would only take one egg from any nest I found. I was very proud of my collection, which I kept in shoeboxes with cotton wool spread around the bottom and sides to protect the delicate shells. I would gladly regale visitors to our house with the story behind each acquisition, no doubt occasionally boasting of the dangers and risks overcome to obtain some prizes.

Sometimes my egg-hunting led to further adventures. There used to be the remains of a castle in the woods;

these remains are probably gone now. I found a jackdaw's nest in one of the chimney pots. The chimney was unfortunately too narrow to allow me access to the nest, but jackdaw's eggs were a comparative rarity, partly because these birds usually nested in the upper reaches of tall trees, so in my eager pursuit of such a prize I lowered my brother Pat down to get one of the eggs.

Unfortunately, Pat got stuck and began to panic, and only after much frenzied pushing and pulling did I manage to get him out of his predicament, but most importantly, he brought the coveted jackdaw's egg with him. As far as I can remember after all these years, it was a blue egg with black spots.

Robins' eggs were equally hard to come by, although I eventually managed to acquire one as well, plus a swan's egg, which, as you might imagine, was quite large. Yellowhammer eggs were very hard to find too. If we were fortunate enough to find a magpie's nest it would invariably be full of scraps of silver paper, as magpies are attracted to shiny objects, for some reason.

Looking back I'm surprised at how much I must have learned about different birds and their habits, and I doubt if many kids today have as much contact with nature as we did back then, before the days of television, video and sophisticated computer games.

There was a bounty on foxes, which meant that if you could bring a brush (or in some areas a tongue) to the local garda station they'd give you ten shillings (50p). So we'd crawl around on our bellies in the undergrowth, somehow imagining we'd one day capture a fox and earn the reward, not merely for the sake of adventure but because we seriously needed the money at home.

Those woods had an added benefit for us kids in that you would rarely see an adult in the vicinity. Most men had some kind of job, no matter how lowly, and women were usually busy in their houses, so it would be rare to have adults out and about anyway. But if one was spotted, no matter how far away, you either hid or ran, but either way you kept out of their way until they'd well gone. They had no part in our private, magical world.

It seemed perfectly safe to roam around in the open, even at that early age. That's something which, sadly, is more difficult to do today in our more threatening society. Drugs were unheard-of then, so much so that I can recall once hearing about (but not actually seeing) a purple heart, a heart-shaped amphetamine tablet which later became very popular.

More often than not I'd go down to the woods on my own, whereas some of the other kids were more inclined to hang about in their own small gangs. Sometimes I'd remain in the woods all day, until it was time to go home to bed. At other times I'd be with Pat or a kid called Eddie. All in all it was a very healthy way of life for a child, living so close to nature and out in the fresh air for so much of the time at such a formative age. Playing in the woods was also a means of postponing my anxiety about homework, which I'd most likely end up doing in bed or at the last minute on the way to school the following day.

Anxiety over homework, money and food for the table were not the only serious concerns occupying my young mind at the time. Clothes, too, were often far too expensive in our straitened circumstances, but we were not alone in this. We'd get our shoes, for example, from a popular place called The Tuckers off Parnell Street, where a second-hand pair, which was just about all we could afford, would cost two shillings. I must say that none of us ever had to go barefoot, but with all my rambling through the woods and climbing trees my shoes never lasted long enough for me to pass them on to Pat.

None of us were remotely concerned with any sense of fashion or trends in clothes then. I don't think I was aware of anything in that line until drainpipe trousers and Teddy-boy haircuts came in after Elvis Presley and the rockers became popular. Generally the clothes you wore, or what others wore, barely cost you a thought. Clothes were merely something to keep you warm and dry. Cheap plastic sandals would not have earned a second glance. Today they would from part of some complex fashion statement.

But a place like Parnell Street in the centre of Dublin was quite a long distance away from home. The only other time we might go that far into the city centre was if we took a bus in to buy bangers (small noisy explosives, not sausages!). They were illegal, but we knew there was a flat in Mary's Mansions where you could buy them and if I had some money left over from some money-making exploit I might make a purchase.

Getting into the city meant a bus ride but money was so scarce that many people would make the journey on foot in order to save the couple of pence. Where we lived was then virtually on the border between the city and the countryside, long before the growth of urban development pushed the countryside further out.

We were more likely to head off in the other direction, to Dublin Airport, which back then was little more than that one small building with a distinctive green watch-tower above the main terminal. I think that the original building is still there, virtually lost among the modern developments around it. The airport had one shop downstairs and a soft-drinks machine, which was a major attraction to us kids. There was a balcony upstairs, around which you could roam at leisure. The whole airport was very different from the extensive complex with tight security it became in later years. Another novelty on the balcony were the mounted binoculars, into which you put threepence and got a great close-up view of the planes. We could rarely afford the few pence for it, but sometimes, if you were lucky and quick, you might be able to grab one after the previous user had left it with a little time outstanding. Although it was probably about five miles from our house I often walked out to the airport in the evening. I'm not sure if too many kids today would walk five miles for anything.

If we took the number three bus in the opposite direction we could get right to the wall beside Sandymount beach. My mother took us there many times as kids, with pre-prepared sandwiches in a cardboard box. A shilling would get you a pot of boiling water for tea from a house near the strand, although since I was usually commissioned to go for the water and would invariably get distracted, by the time I'd get back the sandwiches would be full of sand. We'd all stay there for the whole day, fascinated by an environment so different from our suburban home.

I used to go to a barber shop near the Viscount Bar on the Swords Road whenever my mother decided I needed a haircut and there was money to spare to pay for it. During one visit the barber, Mr Finnegan, accidentally cut the back of my neck and I ran all the way home and told my mother, 'Mr Finnegan cut the back of my neck with his razor and he was singing "Love Letters in the Sand" at the time.' I've no idea why the fact that he was singing the popular hit song of the fifties seemed so significant, but it obviously made a deep impression on me. Maybe I felt that he should have been concentrating on his job and not entertaining us with his repertoire.

Stealing apples was another regular activity in our area – as in many others. On one occasion myself and Pat and some other kids were out on a raid of a local orchard. Even though I was only two years older than my brother I use to boss him around, and I gave him strict instructions on this expedition that if we were spotted we were to drop the apples and run. When the man who owned the orchard appeared unexpectedly somebody gave the pre-arranged signal 'LOB' (meaning 'Look out, boys!') and we all dropped our stash of apples from under our jumpers and legged it as fast as we could. Pat and I headed for a barbed-wire fence, which I got over fairly easily, but Pat, being a chubby lad, could only struggle through it, and in the course of doing so he tore a nasty lump out of his leg.

I managed to get him home while holding the insides of his leg, which looked like spaghetti to me, together with a handkerchief. When I got near our house I ran ahead screaming, 'Mammy, Mammy, Pat's coming up the road with his guts hanging out.' My unfortunate choice of words nearly gave her a heart attack, but in due course both she and Pat recovered.

There were some clubs in the area, like the Home Farm Football Club, but I grew up in a household which did not encourage you to join clubs, not least because the money was not available to buy such essentials as football boots or whatever equipment might be needed. Perhaps as a result I've never been too interested in sports, except thet later in Daingean I played a little Gaelic football and when I was in prison I took up boxing – but more to relieve the boredom than as part of any commitment to the sports themselves.

I don't recall ever going to Dublin Zoo, with which most other Dublin kids were probably very familiar, but we had an annual visit to our locality from a carnival, and that was a major event. For some reason I can remember a priest coming into our classroom each year after the carnival and asking us how much we'd spent at the carnival and how much our parents had spent. He would compliment those in the class who could claim impressive figures, maybe ten shillings or more. I've never understood why it mattered to him what we spent, unless it was a neat way of finding out which households had money to spare and whom he might then chase for extra church donations. Of course for kids whose parents could not afford to spend much money on such a comparatively frivolous luxury it was a real embarrassment.

That deep sense of not being able to take part in things like most other kids was a constant companion in my early years. When, as a kid, I accidentally wandered into a Boy Scouts hall early one bright evening it brought out all my sense of disappointment and my perpetual feelings of not being good enough, seeing them all dressed up in their uniforms, happy and busy and excitedly preparing for their summer holidays. They had a big map up on a blackboard while the Scoutmaster explained to them where they were going and how much money they would need. Then they all sang the jolly German marching song 'I Love to Go A-Wandering' while I just stood there feeling totally excluded and inferior and miserable, and that profound effect still lives inside me to this day, the sense of somehow not being worthy or deserving.

Even a visit to the Grand Cinema was a great novelty, to such an extent that I can still clearly remember the first time my father took me there. A local character called Harry the Weed was on the door and all I can remember of the film was seeing this enormous brown horse up on the big screen.

The only other local character was a harmless chap we called Hairy Lemon. Hairy Lemon always wore an enormous heavy overcoat and a huge beard, and he'd go around from door to door begging for some bread and jam, a cup of tea or a few pence.

Going door-to-door was quite a common practice during my childhood and I did it myself regularly. For example, if you collected enough old rags you could swap them for little brown bags with sticks of rock sweets, or jam jars could be traded for pieces of that stuff that you get inside Crunchie bars. You could swap things for little pieces of pink sweets that had white powder on them and which I seem to remember we called 'lucky lumps' because sometimes you'd win a threepenny piece in one.

A shop beside the Grand Cinema would sell you half a toffee for a halfpenny. They'd also sell you half a cigarette if you couldn't afford a whole one! When you were really flush you could buy an ice cream. Depending on whether you wanted a twopenny, fourpenny or sixpenny one, the shopkeeper would take out this marker which would indicate where he should slice the ice-cream, then he'd put two wafers around it and you'd be delighted with your treat.

There was little live music in the Dublin of those days, not even in pubs, many of which actually forbade singing and even displayed stern notices saying 'No Singing Allowed on these Premises'. The only music, apart from what I heard on the radio, would have been when my parents or a neighbour would organise a hooley and friends would come around, and they'd drink and sing and eat sandwiches. That was the height of in-house entertainment in the days before television, video, computer games and records took over most households and more or less banished live entertainment to the pubs and concert halls and discos.

Even if you had a radio there was only one Irish station, Radio Éireann, but it used to close down at about three o'clock in the afternoons, ending its broadcast with a dull voice calling out the runners for the following day's Irish race meeting. The station would go off the air until early evening and close again at midnight until eight the next morning.

But I suppose it would be fair to say that while inside our house there was much trouble and turmoil, my life outdoors was probably little different from that of thousands of other working-class kids of my era. There was probably less crime, with fewer serious burglaries and thefts, but then people had little that was worth stealing anyway. When kids were caught stealing apples it was treated almost as something to be expected from kids anyway, and at worst you might get a clip on the ear, whereas today such incidents would probably swell the crime statistics and inspire university theses.

Working men would bring sandwiches, and perhaps a flask of tea, with them to work each day. Generally only the men went out to work, although a hard-pressed wife might take a part-time job cleaning another woman's house if she could deal with the stigma of poverty that was attached to such menial work. There were no female bus drivers or conductors. There might have been a small number of women teachers, and our school inspector was female. A key part of your average housewife's chores first thing in the morning or last thing at night was to prepare the lunch for her husband to take with him to his place of work. Eating out was unheard of for people like us, even in a cheap café, of which there were very few anyway, although we were fortunate that the school provided some food for us each day.

Life was simpler, and probably far more innocent, back then, and there were many bright moments in my childhood, even if underlying it all I was battling with my own private demons.

5

THE SURROGATE FAMILY

In a normal family, which ours never was, there comes a time for a young boy to transfer his central focus from his mother to his father in order to start learning his role as a man. A boy at first seeks acceptance and love from his mother, but when the time comes he will shift that focus to fit his need to establish his growth towards manhood.

In turn, a boy then needs a male role model in order to develop a natural and fulfilling emotional life. He has to learn a mode of behaviour and a language that reinforce his identity as a male, but without losing contact with his mother.

According to the clinical psychologist Oliver J. Killeen, 'Research shows that when fathers are actively involved in the lives of their sons they turn out to be less aggressive and better able to express their feelings of vulnerability. The closer the emotional bond between fathers and sons is, the lower the incidence of social delinquency.'

Those normal growth patterns, unfortunately, were

never possible in our domestic circumstances. Quite the reverse, in fact, especially for the older two, my sister Catherine and me. Because of the increasing difficulties created for the children by the daily acrimony between our parents, Catherine became our surrogate mother, trying to keep the home together, cleaning, cooking and so on, while I, as the older boy, became the surrogate father, acting as the breadwinner. Our assumption of these roles was purely instinctive and driven by the simple need to provide for ourselves.

Even though our parents still lived with us, to all intents and purposes we were emotionally abandoned, especially by my father, who was rarely there, and when he was around he would be either drunk or in a foul temper.

Meanwhile my mother had begun to treat me almost totally like an adult, always expecting me to act responsibly, despite my young years. I was later to suffer from having that burden placed on me before I was mature enough to cope with it. Little did I know then but this was actually setting me up for the co-dependency I suffered later in life. I know that Catherine too still has a lot of pain inside her from that time, although she did not develop addictive tendencies to the extent that I did.

Our brother Pat became very quiet, although because Catherine and I effectively took the roles of his parents he was able to enjoy a more normal childhood. So he played football and was much like other kids of that era and social class. Breda, our youngest sister at that stage, recalls almost nothing of those times. Whether the trials and tribulations simply did not register with her or whether some inner defence mechanism has deliberately suppressed these memories, it's impossible for me to say.

During one spell in hospital I used to attend the hospital school every day, and one day my mother arrived with my new books. It was the practice at that time to cover new school books with wallpaper to protect the covers, but when I looked at the covers of my new books I noticed the wallpaper was smeared with candle grease. When I asked my mother about this she explained that the electricity had been cut off in the house because the bill had not been paid. This brought on a spasm of fretting over the plight of the family. The circumstances my brother and sisters were in could bring me to shed tears, but sadly I was incapable of doing that for myself.

So when I was released from hospital I responded to our immediate plight with total commitment. I watched out for every opportunity, no matter how small, to help out. I'd go down to the Brother sewing-machine factory and take boxes, which I'd carry home, chop into neat bundles, put elastic bands around and sell door-to-door for a penny a bundle. In the days before every home could afford firelighters, mothers would be delighted to get a bundle of kindling to help get a fire going.

I collected jam jars and sold them to get money to

buy food. I robbed orchards, 'boxing the fox', as we called it, and I'd sell the apples at five for a shilling (5p in to-day's money). I helped the grocery man on Saturdays. I'd get up at three o'clock on cold wintry mornings to work on a milk round. I did anything to bring in the badly needed shillings.

So I was far from lazy and took on whatever I could in order to provide for the family, although I had no idea that our real problem stemmed from my father's relentless drinking. When I collected the weekly payments from the people on my paper round I could sense that, even though there might not be any signs of great wealth, there was a pleasant warmth and friend-liness emanating from their houses. I'd envy the cosiness I felt from my stolen glimpses inside those houses when they left the door ajar while fetching the money. How different from my own cold, unfeeling battleground of a home.

Our kind of poverty results not only in a lack of regular meals, but in poor nutrition, so we were prone to colds and infections. Periodically I suffered badly from earaches and I'd wake to find patches of awful pus all over the pillow, but I had to suffer on regardless. We couldn't afford a doctor or the appropriate medicine from a chemist.

Needless to say, we couldn't afford a car. Our television, when we had one, worked on a slot system, and we had a battered old radio. But it was not material wealth that we missed. People in the fifties, and even into the sixties in working-class Dublin, had few of the luxuries we take for granted today and were not necessarily less happy without them. But most important of all we lacked the one thing money can't buy – love.

Later, when I attended therapy sessions, I was amazed to see clearly outlined on a blackboard the various ways in which families react to the kind of situations we found ourselves in and to find that we had followed the established patterns almost to the letter. I was absolutely stunned when I found that other people knew about this stuff and, such was the accuracy of their detailed knowledge, that I even suspected that one of them must have been in our house when I was a kid, so graphically did they reflect what had happened to me at home. It was clear they understood exactly how our situation had developed and that it was nothing new, and certainly not unique to the Baker family.

One way families typically deal with such internal problems is to elect a 'scapegoat' or a 'lost child'. I also learned how you can have the 'hero', who is usually the oldest, like me. This doesn't really mean you're a hero in the normal sense of the word, but you're more likely to be angry and get into serious trouble, perhaps using hard drugs or turning to crime, as you take on responsibilty for the others in the family, a responsibilty you are really too young to shoulder.

The 'lost child' is the one who melts into the furniture, staying so quiet you'd hardly know he or she is around. In our family, that was my younger sister Breda. You can have the 'caretaker', like my sister Catherine, who tries to handle the providing role, perhaps down to hiding a little sugar or butter for later on, when it might be even more scarce, and taking the traditional role of the mother in Irish homes.

Part of me was a caretaker too, forever on the lookout for odd jobs that would earn money or for discarded items we could use in the house. By talking responsibility for somebody else, the 'caretaker' helps himself by alleviating his own pain. It's another form of the 'people-pleasing' which dogged me for much of my later life.

I played bits of all those roles, driven by an intense survival instinct, a desire to see us through somehow or other. But you could talk to five members of the same family and hear five different stories, as if they were all members of different families, because the different roles they each assume gives each of them an altered view of the overall situation.

So while I was to be permanently scarred by the experience, neither my brother nor sisters were, because to all intents and purposes they were experiencing a different family from me in practical terms. As the eldest, there was nobody for me to turn to at all, but at least they had me, an older brother, fighting on their behalf and looking out for them as much as I could. I recently inadvertently referred to my brother Pat as 'my son'. Was it a Freudian slip or a meaningless mistake?

I'll never know, but I think it sheds a little light on the family scenario and our adopted roles within it.

Of course it's grossly unreasonable that any child should have to try to take on the role of an adult, but in certain situations like ours there may be no alternative. But the circumstances in which I grew up left me with enormous emotional and psychological problems all stemming from my childhood, perhaps because in reality I never had a real childhood at all.

6

Rebel with a Cause

I can't recall ever feeling any real sense of prolonged happiness at any time during those years of domestic turmoil in Whitehall. Instead, I was emotionally abandoned by my parents, and to add to my woes I had started to cause serious trouble myself. I have since assumed that the two were linked.

Initially it was just the usual stuff. Because Whitehall was closer to the countryside then than it is now, I'd mitch from school, hide my school bag in a ditch and go off for the day chasing horses. When I caught one I'd ride it bareback round a field for hours, exhilarated by the sense of freedom and the contact with nature. I even suffered a nasty fall once when a horse kicked me in the back during one such escapade.

There was a popular television series at the time called *Have Gun Will Travel*. So some of my school teachers took to referring to me as 'have bag will travel' on account of my tendency to carry my school bag in an unorthodox fashion, more like a gunslinger in a western film, and because I'd run off whenever the opportunity arose.

Sometimes I'd arrive home to be told by one of my sisters that my mother had found out about me mitching, so I'd immediately take off again – 'go on gur', as we used to call it, and I'd sleep rough for a couple of nights, maybe in someone's back shed, until it was time to get up and help the milkman or move on to avoid getting caught. Of course I'd be afraid, sleeping out on my own overnight, but I'd try to act the tough guy as part of my new persona.

But while such behaviour might be written off as mere pranks by a wilful child growing up in troubled circumstances, I soon moved on to more serious matters. In a lengthy series of misdemeanours I broke into the local school and nearby houses, thieved and caused damage to property.

I believe this errant behaviour was my way of testing my parents. I wanted them to come after me, to show they cared about me, to get me out of the scrapes I got myself into. I wanted their attention and their love. In fact I still behave like that today, testing people if I'm in a relationship with them, although it's a habit I only latterly became aware of. But there's a clear pattern in my later behaviour that relates directly back to a lot of what happened in my early life.

An unfeeling cruelty had crept into my behaviour back then too. This was perhaps at its worst when I killed a cat stone-dead one day. I waited quietly behind a gate, watched its shadow approaching and killed it with a vicious crack from a hurling stick. It frightens me today to think that I could have perpetrated such cruelty on an innocent, defenceless animal for absolutely no gain. Even more disturbing, in the wake of this dreadful act I felt not a single hint of remorse or guilt, no feelings whatsoever as far as I can remember, and I simply carried on playing about with my mates as if nothing of consequence had happened.

During another escapade I broke into the local school, poured paint all over the piano, smashed bottles up and down the hallway with a golf stick and turned on all the taps, leaving the basins to overflow and flood the floors. This wasn't so much an anti-school action as the outpouring of an uncontainable anger welling up within me. I felt like an outcast, so I behaved like an outcast. Being good, as I was when I devoted so much energy to helping the family, didn't get me anywhere and didn't fix anything. I felt lost and lonely, so I acted tough. It got so bad that the authorities recommended I see a psychiatrist or a psychologist to see if they could help me deal with my uncontrollable rage. This suggestion itself only served to fuel my anger. Why was my behaviour being questioned in this way? Why was nobody asking my father or my mother about what was going on in the home? Why was I being picked on? Why did nobody suggest that my father see a doctor instead of me?

As a result of my committing a string of petty crimes I was summoned before the courts several times, but with one excuse or another I managed to get off each time. But then at the age of twelve came the inevitable occasion when at last my luck ran out and I was due to appear in court as the result of my latest misdemeanour.

I now had to face the fact that matters had taken a very serious turn. It was made clear to me that the authorities were losing patience with me and it was practically certain that they were going to put me away this time, no matter what lies or excuses I came up with.

The day before the court hearing my da came up with a clever plan. After deliberately cutting his finger he carefully wiped the blood on part of his handkerchief. He then told me to spit on his handkerchief, took a matchstick and mixed his blood with my spittle. He then took me down to the Mater Hospital, told the doctor of my history of TB and my hospital visits, and produced the 'evidence' on his handkerchief that convinced them I'd been coughing up blood. In fairness to my father the ruse worked perfectly and I was taken into hospital in Blanchardstown immediately, thus depriving the court of the opportunity of sending me away. Unfortunately my joy at escaping an almost-certain sentence in one of the many institutions for young offenders dotted around the country was short-lived.

When I arrived back in the hospital, the same one for the third time, I discovered to my anger that they'd reversed the boy-girl units again and I was now heading back to the unit where I'd suffered so much anxiety on my first visit six years previously. I was soon overcome with abject terror, which was further complicated by the fact that I had no understanding of why I felt so scared, having blocked my previous traumatic experience from my memory. I was like a kid who had nearly drowned and who is afraid to go near water but doesn't know the reason for his fear because he can't remember having been nearly drowned.

At the hospital they repeatedly asked me to explain my reluctance to go into the boys' unit. I angrily screamed at them to put me somewhere, anywhere, other than the unit that held so much dread for me, but I couldn't explain why. I was so terrified that I ached to return to the familiarity of my home surroundings, despite all the unpleasantness I had suffered there.

On the first night in the hospital I waited for the usual drill of the nurse coming around at about eleven o'clock to check on all the patients. After I knew she'd done her duty I took my clothes and climbed out through the window, forded a little river close to the hospital and hitched a lift from a passing motorist, who took me back towards my home some miles away.

When I reached our house I clambered up a drainpipe at the back and made my way inside my room. But my relief at being back in familiar surroundings was interrupted by the arrival ten minutes later of the police with the news for my parents that I was missing from the hospital and that they were combing the area for me. None of them realised I was tucked up in my own bed upstairs!

After I was discovered next day my mother told me I'd either have to go back to hospital or face the courts and the risk of being sentenced to time in an institution, so I reluctantly opted to return to the hospital. She dropped me back there, but this time, instead of the dreaded boys' unit from which I'd fled, I was put into unit twelve with the male adults. It could have been so much worse.

7

ANOTHER HOME TO GO TO

When I was finally discharged after my third stay in Blanchardstown Hospital a number of unwelcome surprises were awaiting me. The first bombshell came when my mother announced that we would have to live somewhere else. We'd fallen so far behind with our rent payments to Dublin Corporation that we were being evicted from the house in Whitehall and given alternative accommodation in a flat in Corporation Buildings in Corporation Street, a short walk from O'Connell Street in the heart of Dublin.

By this time of the actual move my parents had split up. My mother had had enough of my father's drinking and living with the constant threat of violence and had simply run away and taken my brother Pat with her. Their first night had been spent huddled together in a park beside Whitehall Church.

Meanwhile, my two sisters, Catherine and Breda, were placed in the Sacred Heart Home in Drumcondra, where they were to remain for years. This was a truly disturbing development for them and a devastating blow for both Pat and me, causing me much anxiety. Given my assumed role as the father figure, it was like having my own children taken away from me.

Just before we moved into the flat in Corporation Street my mother warned us not to be upset by what we were about to find there, but her words did little to prepare me for the shock of discovering what was to pass as our new 'home', which we would also have to share with her current lover, Joey. But then nothing would have prepared me for it. There was tin sheeting on the windows instead of glass. There was no gas, no electricity, just one room with a filthy toilet, one grubby wash-hand basin, and one cold tap. That single room had to accommodate two adults and two children. The only pieces of furniture were two beds and a dresser. Because the windows were blocked up we had to use candles to provide us with light even in the daytime.

The streets outside were littered with papers and rags, and both human and dog excrement was smeared all over the pavements and hallways; the smell of urine was so prevalent you didn't notice it after a while. Our previous home was mere purgatory compared to this hell.

The flat was basically a slum which was situated in such a dangerous area that it was known locally as 'the cage'. Every night there would be several fights, both inside the buildings and outside, to a level we had never experienced in Whitehall. For the first few weeks I was involved in about three serious fist fights every day. I was the new kid on the block, so I had to be tested, and I in turn had to make sure they knew I could look after myself and wouldn't take any nonsense. 'You don't fuck with me, and you don't fuck with any member of my family,' was the message I had to send out loud and clear if I wanted to survive in this daunting environment. As a result, I was continually disfigured – a bloody nose yesterday, a black eye today, a busted lip tomorrow, a torn cheek the day after. My acts of violence under these circumstances were intended purely to protect my family rather than for any reasons of badmindedness, although I can understand if some find it hard to see it that way.

After a couple of days the authorities replaced the tin sheeting on the windows with glass, as a major concession to us as we tried to turn this appalling hovel into a home. Meanwhile, my own response to our new level of deprivation was to go out and steal money from the nearby CIE office in O'Connell Street. I walked calmly back into the flat, placed a hundred pounds – a lot of money in those days – on the mantelpiece, and casually walked back out again. My career as a serious criminal had begun.

We had further grief with the news that my father had emigrated to England, where he had subsequently been taken ill. He had to be hospitalised over there. Missing my sisters dreadfully, the shock of these further downturns in our fortunes forced me to block out my true feelings so as to enable me to get on with the difficult business of surviving and helping the others to survive.

But fate was not finished with us yet, and to add further to our woes my mother discovered she was pregnant. Then, without warning, my father arrived back from England. When he saw my mother's new domestic arrangement his anger flared and he tackled her lover-boy Joey in a pub in Talbot Street. Joey was so frightened by my father that he ran, simply took off, never to be seen again by any of us.

When my mother's time came she gave birth to triplets, all boys. Sadly, all three of them died at birth, but my reaction to that tragedy added another layer to my guilt. It's probably the thing in my life of which I am now most thoroughly ashamed, but I actually felt glad the babies had died, although I still feel pained that I could have allowed myself to feel that way.

Presumably, given the difficulties with which we were already having to cope, I was most concerned as to how the babies were going to be fed, clothed and cared for in what was already an overcrowded situation. We had hardly enough food for ourselves, never mind three more innocent mouths. It was that fear that sparked my uncharitable reaction to their deaths.

I never knew how my mother felt about losing the three babies she'd carried in her womb through nine months of upheaval. I never thought to ask her, then or later. I also felt a sense of shame towards my mother like I'd never felt shame before. Today I understand why she may have been driven to leave my father, since she too had to find a way of surviving the trials he visited upon her. It was probably inevitable, too, since she was clearly starved for love and attention from a husband who was out drinking most of the time, hardly ever at home and in bad humour when he was and unable to provide for his family in the traditional way expected of fathers in those days.

But, irrespective or her motivations and feelings and my rational understanding of them now, her infidelity has made it almost impossible for me to trust completely any woman with whom I have been in a serious, committed relationship. During your most impressionable years your mother represents all women in the world to you, and if she betrays you, or the family, you begin to feel that maybe every woman is like that. That's an unfair burden to lay upon any one person, since we are all prone to making mistakes of one kind or another, but it seems to be the way human nature works.

For me to trust a woman is still such a very difficult task, and as I am aware that without complete trust a fulfilling relationship is virtually impossible to sustain, I long to enjoy a successful relationship with a woman without that terrifying fear of abandonment or betrayal. And all of that goes back to my relationship with my own mother.

But I was angry with my father too. When first he arrived back in Dublin after his move to England I wanted to attack him because I was so angered by what he'd done to all of us, but especially what he'd done to our mother. But I was also old enough to know he still had major problems of his own and was finding it difficult, if not impossible, to deal with them. With his reputation for drinking and his recent health problems he was finding it very difficult to get work anywhere in Dublin, although in some respects that was almost a blessing in disguise, since at least it meant he had less money to squander on drink.

Consequently his drinking problems were far less acute than they had been, and although we were now living in one room our life was at least preferable to the bad old days in that respect. We were a sort of family again, albeit under the most difficult circumstances, and my sisters were still kept away from us.

Unfortunately the enforced reduction in the intake of alcohol did not solve many of my father's troubles. Without access to drink he'd regularly become more violently angry than ever, and that often caused increased pain for all his family, which, following Joey's departure, had been increased by the arrival of another baby, my third and youngest sister, Ada, born in 1969.

Despite my own deep-felt anger, I'd never spoken out against the treatment we'd all been subjected to at home, not just the beatings and the threats of worse to follow, but the lack of care and love. But when I got a bit older, perhaps around the age of thirteen, I began to develop a resentment about what I'd been through, and I blamed my father for most of it.

I'd given up going to school after my last visit to hospital, so I took a succession of odd jobs here and there, anything for a few shillings to buy food or to pay the electricity bill. But I was always unable to resist the opportunity of stealing from my employers. For instance, I worked for a short while in a clothing factory called Lathams at the end of Mary Street. My job entailed pushing a handcart laden with bales of cloth through the streets from one factory to another, until the inevitable happened – I was caught selling bales of stolen cotton and had to move on.

To all intents and purposes I was serving my apprenticeship as a criminal. I knew stealing was wrong, but I had to do something to help my family to survive, given that my father was incapable of doing – or unwilling to do – his duty. Rather than spend any more time than absolutely necessary in the stultifying surroundings of our 'home', I'd fill my spare hours roaming around the streets of Dublin, casually casing places to burgle and eyeing the world and all the people in it with a barely concealed loathing.

8

HELL-HOUND ON MY TRAIL

If you commit enough crimes, the inevitable happens.
Throughout my early teens I was in and out of court
on so many theft charges that I lost count. Sooner or
later the courts tire of hearing lame excuses and empty
promises to mend their ways from those repeatedly up
before them. I was not destined to be treated any
differently from hundreds of others and was remanded
for a month in Marlborough House for my latest act of
thievery.

With frightening predictability, the crippling anxiety
I'd felt during my stays in hospital came back to haunt
me again. I tried to convince myself – foolishly, I must
now confess – that I had grown more resilient and was
now man enough, despite not even having become a
teenager, to deal with my inner fears. Raised on a diet
of John Wayne movies and the traditional role of men
in Irish society, I had begun to act the tough guy and
thought I could handle anything. But this was only a
means of hiding my true feelings from everybody,
including myself.

It was hardly surprising that the authorities finally had enough and decided to send me down. But one thing sticks out in my memory about one of the many cops who had been involved in my arrests and eventual trial. When I walked into a room at Alcoholics Anonymous about twenty years later I was greeted by that same man, who recognised me, offered me a cup of tea and said 'Welcome'. I looked into his face during that unexpected meeting and felt a deep resentment for the part he'd paid in my tribulations, yet here he was, a struggling alcoholic like myself. In time I lost some of that resentment, yet I have to admit I still cannot bring myself to like the man who played, as I saw it, such an active role on my road to self-destruction.

I was subsequently sentenced to two years in the notorious reform school at Daingean, although it would be more accurate and honest to describe it as a prison. Nothing in my life up to that time had even remotely prepared me for the horrors that this loveless and hate-filled place brought to me and many others. Here I was in a remote part of the Irish midlands, far removed from the people and places that were familiar to me, a scared teenager cast among strangers who cared nothing for me, and with nobody to turn to for help or understanding. The sense of bewildering abandonment I'd felt on that first visit to hospital when I was six would in due course be reinforced, and then some, by my stay in this dreadful place.

I was allowed to bring nothing with me to Daingean

except the clothes on my back, but even those were stripped from me immediately on my arrival and replaced with horrible rags that didn't even fit me.

I was incarcerated there for nearly two years and at the age of about thirteen I began to suffer major anxiety attacks which were of the kind that normally happen to adults. From this anxiety I developed a twitch in one of my eyes. I couldn't allow anything or anyone to touch my neck or my back. I've since read that Jewish survivors of the Holocaust have a similar fear. Of course I don't want to suggest, not even for a second, that my suffering was on a par with that meted out by Hitler's murderers, but the fear of someone touching you on the back, even accidentally, seems to be common among those who've suffered oppressive incarceration.

I soon developed the habit of constantly fixing my shirt at the back of my pants. I couldn't sit or stand still, I had to keep moving, as if trying to escape the trail of suffering which I knew was bound to catch up with me sooner or later. Looking back from the comparative safety of adulthood I'm sure I must have been close at times to a complete mental breakdown. Decades later, a rash sometimes breaks out on the back of my neck from nerves caused by the bullying that went on in that hell-hole.

As if my previous troubles at home were not enough, the mental torture visited upon me by some of the Oblate Brothers who ran Daingean was something you would have to live through to fully understand, yet these men professed to be Christian brothers and priests.

One particular brother there was a paedophile. Intuitively I knew this, although intellectually I had no idea that such people existed. He made a concerted effort to groom me as a potential victim, to break me down so that he could use me for his evil pleasures.

To protect myself I instinctively chose to act as innocently as I could. As part of his plan he gave me a job working in the church that formed part of the dour, daunting surroundings. I'm sure it was no accident that my duties meant I would spend much of my time on my own, isolated from the other inmates, so that he could prey on me. When he'd arrive down to supervise me he'd make the most suggestive comments, like, 'Did you go hard today?' and 'Did you have an erection?'

I'd pretend I'd no idea what he meant by these questions. At that age most children in Catholic Ireland would have had only a very hazy notion what he was referring to, although they would probably suspect that it was something sinful and 'dirty'. I cannot remember hearing a single word of explanation about sexual matters from either of my parents, or any teachers or priests while I was growing up, and I reckon that this was equally true of the vast majority of Irish children of the fifties and sixties. But maybe that ignorance helped me keep up the façade of innocence that seemed to keep him at bay from day to day.

This dreadful creature would persist with his suggestive talk almost every time our paths crossed, which was often, but whatever he said I'd pretend not to understand. After my mother's monthly visit he'd sidle up to me and slyly say things like, 'Did you see any girls visiting?' Again I'd play innocent. I'd pretend to think very hard and I'd tell him, 'Well, I saw Tommy's little sister.' He'd say, 'No, that's not what I mean. Did you see any older girls?' I'd say I hadn't noticed any and he'd ask me had I not noticed this particular girl and did I not feel an erection when I saw her. He'd ask me had I touched myself or allowed any of the other boys to touch me.

One day I was taken on a rare trip away from the environs of the school. I went to the town of Tullamore in a truck with him to collect doors which were to be used in the reform school for partitioning one of the halls. He tried to put his hand on my balls while we were in the truck. This truly shocked and frightened me, but when I opened the door to jump out he pretended he was only joking.

No matter how much he kept on about it I stubbornly refused to give in to him, although others less fortunate did give in. He was only one of many brothers who were up to the same disgusting, devious tricks. I knew there was something wrong about it, although I didn't know exactly what. Paedophilia was not something that had entered the range of my experience on any level up to that time. I'd probably heard men referred to as 'dirty old men', without quite knowing what that term meant. But then all my teachers had been of the lay variety and this was my first, and fortunately last, encounter with men belonging to a religious order.

In Daingean I saw boys being viciously beaten up by the brothers all the time. In one particularly bad instance, but unfortunately one of many, a certain brother, of whom all of the boys were terrified, approached a boy called Bonzo Downey from Sheriff Street in Dublin's inner city who was sitting beside me in the refectory. The brother spoke a few threatening words to him, then he took off the large, heavy crucifix which was part of his religious garb and, without warning, cracked Downey's head open with it. Downey fell to the floor unconscious before the brother dragged him outside and off to be taken care of.

It was the culture of such places never to allow yourself to show any outward signs of real fear or hurt. Although we were all in our teens, we were expected, and expected each other, to accept whatever inhuman indignities, abuse and pain was inflicted upon us, as if we were all tough men, hardened enough to handle anything this awful life could throw at us. In truth this was a highly dangerous way for us to try to cope with such barbaric treatment.

I've often tried to figure out what went on in the minds of these cruel men, but I still have no real understanding of them. These were, after all, assumed by us to be our religious betters. I, and my fellow inmates, were supposed to learn how to become better Christians and better citizens from their teachings and by their example, yet they behaved like the most animalistic thugs every day, from morning till night. At the time I rationalised the treatment I received as part of my punishment – another great mistake on my part, as it only reinforced my feelings of guilt and low self-worth.

I came across a theory recently to the effect that paedophiles are often attracted to young boys with an angelic countenance and I reckon I would have fitted that description when I was that age. Maybe that is a partial explanation, but it still remains a puzzle to me as to why I was singled out for the kind of persistent sexual attention that others did not seem to receive.

Initially one might be inclined to assume that the degree of cruelty meted out to young children by religious supervisors resulted from the mere badness of a few isolated individuals. But the widespread and almost uniform nature of the harsh treatment meted out to young people in schools, reform institutions and even in family homes suggests something far more deeply ingrained in Irish society. Equally sadly, I have often suspected that some acts of cruelty were occasions of pleasure, perhaps even of a sexual nature, to the perpetrators.

It puzzles me that, despite the volume of accusations and convictions and the body of evidence produced in the courts and by other sources, confirming that the most awful crimes were committed by some Catholic priests and brothers, the Catholic Church has not conducted an investigation to find an explanation. After all, the scandal is likely to do enormous damage to the image of the Catholic religion and Christianity in general, apart altogether from the damage to the individuals involved.

For me personally, the climax of the abuse came when three of the brothers, including the vicious paedophile, flogged me. They took me down from my dormitory, three burly adults against one child, stripped me bollock-naked, and forced me to kneel on the ground with my hands stretched forward onto a step. One of them stood on my fingers and hands so I couldn't move, as they beat me mercilessly until my legs bled.

I stubbornly refused to cry as they flogged me, aware that the sound of the thrashing was carried out of the cavernous, marbled room to the ears of the other boys, who would themselves quake as they heard each resounding crack. But such stubbornness would also make the brothers more determined to break you, and the treatment I received was not an exceptional example of their frequent brutality towards kids ranging in age from as young as thirteen to sixteen.

We would all have yearned to be able to hit back but their reign of terror was so overwhelming and so absolute we could never dare to take that step. I later heard that some of the inmates were driven to rebel at their treatment and tried to burn the place down, but nothing like that was contemplated, to my knowledge, during my incarceration there.

The paedophile brother mentally tortured me for about fifteen months, but I never once broke, not for a second. He even went so far one day as to accuse me of having kissed a boy in the handball alley, even though I've never had any homosexual tendencies of any kind. If I had, I'd freely admit it, but this was a total fabrication. In spite of my immediate and definite denial he took out a leather strap and crashed it across my face without any warning, advising me to tell the truth. I repeated my denial and started crying, not at the physical pain but at the shameful insinuation that I was sexually interested in other boys.

Amid all this I had to endure all my old recurring feelings of loneliness and rejection, but either I had become even better at handling those feelings or I was more adept at burying them deeper inside me. I now regarded myself as a real man, even though I was only fourteen. Here was another example of the cruel way in which so many Irish childhoods were stolen, for no gain of any kind.

It helped me of course that my mother never missed her monthly visit. Although I enthusiastically looked forward to her visits and to hearing all the news from home, I never again allowed her to get too close to me after that unforgettable time she had left me forlorn and dejected in the hospital. I was terrified of feeling that pain again and I still am to this day.

Yet I was always much closer to her than to my father, who only visited me once in Daingean, and on that occasion he was, typically, drunk. In fact, I suspect he only came because he saw it as a means of getting drink somewhere.

I had originally hoped to get six months' reduction of my time at Daingean for good behaviour, but as a further punishment I was granted a remission of only three months, so in all I spent one year and nine months in that miserable hell-hole before I was released from my torture at the age of fifteen and a half.

9

THE PRISONER

After I came out of Daingean I moved to the Isle of Man and got a job washing dishes in a hotel. It was then that I started drinking seriously. Given my family background and the society I'd grown up in, I thought getting drunk every night was more or less the norm for every man. I also hung around on my own much of the time.

I shared a room with another chap from Dublin's inner city, in separate beds, of course. But one night while I was trying to get to sleep he climbed into bed beside me! I was flabbergasted! When I asked him what he thought he was playing at he said, 'I get lonely sleeping on my own because I usually sleep with my brothers and sisters at home. Do you mind if I sleep with you?'

Although I thought this was more than a bit weird I said OK, but he then put his hands round me and started stroking my balls. With that I jumped out of the bed, had a go at him and told him to fuck off.

One night shortly afterwards he and his mates picked on me outside a pub. I ignored him, but when I went back to the hotel I laid into him and a big brawl ensued. I was later picked up by the police, spent two weeks in an Isle Of Man prison and was deported back to Dublin.

Back in Dublin I resumed my life of thievery. Unfortunately I wasn't much good at it, and the first time I got caught I was sentenced to three months in Saint Patrick's Institution, which I suppose is a Mountjoy Prison for underage offenders and is actually situated right next door to its better-known rival. The next time they caught me I got six months. I got up to so much mischief in those days that I can't even remember exactly what I got sent down for.

Just as I was nearing the end of my six months stint the powers-that-be told me that my fingerprints had been found on incriminating evidence for a number of jobs, and that earned me another nine months. I don't even know whether I was really guilty. I was committing so many thefts and burglaries it hardly mattered whether I was sent down for the right ones or not.

So I was in and out of jail quite a lot for about four years from the age of sixteen. Although I never saw any sign of the drugs which were later to infest the Irish prison system, I saw a lot of real violence in prison, and not just of the sort I'd experienced in Daingean.

In St Patrick's Institution I'd befriended a fellow prisoner called Tony who worked in the prison as a barber. At the same time a chap from Roscommon Waterford called Seamus was serving seven years there for violent crime. One day Seamus demanded that Tony give him a number one, which means shaving the entire head. Tony very politely explained that a number one wouldn't suit Seamus since he didn't have the right shape of head or face to look right when bald and he advised Seamus not to have it done. But Seamus insisted and Tony duly obliged.

But when Seamus looked at himself in a mirror he obviously didn't like what he saw. To avoid making noise with the steel-capped shoes which were regulation wear in prison, he crept on his tiptoes up behind Tony, who was sweeping up the hairs off the floor of his small barber's area. Meanwhile I was up on the third floor with a bucket of water and mop, cleaning up the floor and with a clear view down to the scene below. To my horror I saw Seamus pick up a scissors, grab Tony by the hair and plunge the scissors into his back.

When Tony screamed, two of the prison warders, Punchy Quinn and a guy called Mannix, saw what had happened and ran towards the scene of the incident. This distracted Seamus, who dropped Tony on the ground. With his blood pouring all over the floor, he crawled in agony into one of the nearby cells, and although he was almost paralysed from the stabbing he managed to kick the door shut from the inside. The two screws tried to contain Seamus while I, still up on the third floor, was leaning out over the balcony trying to aim my bucket of water so that it would fall on Seamus's head. But before I could do anything to help he was subdued and taken away.

Doctors arrived from the Mater Hospital and Tony was treated in his cell for about three weeks before he was given a discharge without having to serve the few months remaining on his time. The screws were happy and relieved with that outcome because they were afraid they might forfeit their jobs for allowing such a violent incident to happen while they were on duty. They admitted to me that they feared Tony might make a legal issue of it and put a claim in but, probably through ignorance of his rights, he never did and the incident was forgotten.

Later when I was serving time in Shanganagh Castle near Shankill on the Dublin–Wicklow border, I met a man called Tommy who was serving time for murder. He told me that when he was in St Patrick's the same guy, Seamus, went into Tommy's cell with a sheet of glass and calmly told him he was going to use it on the first person who gave him any trouble.

When Tommy asked him what he hoped to gain from such an act Seamus told him he wanted to do his time in the asylum in Dundrum on the southside of Dublin, where he believed they would sedate him and he'd be able to deal with his violent temper more easily. That explained why he'd gone so viciously for Tony over the haircut row.

Tommy, who was quite an intelligent bloke, managed to persuade him that this ploy would not work, that he'd only provoke the authorities into adding a few more years on to his sentence. But Seamus persevered and eventually I heard that he had succeeded in getting moved to Central Mental Hospital in Dundrum, although one can only speculate as to what action he must have taken in order to achieve this dubious ambition.

Different inmates had different ways of dealing with their problems while in prison, and some, like that chap, found ways, many quite unorthodox and ingenious, of inflicting punishment on themselves. That puzzled me, since I felt we were being punished enough as it was without inflicting more torture on ourselves, but each of us had to find his own way of coping with imprisonment and some found it a much harder task than others.

On another occasion the prisoners were walking around the exercise yard. It being a very chilly day, most of us had our hands shoved firmly down our trouser pockets in an effort to keep warm. The yard had a shed for mops and buckets and the shed had one window. Without the slightest warning, one of the prisoners took his hands out of his pockets, went over to the window and plunged his two arms straight through the glass, causing blood to spout all over the place and over anyone unfortunate enough to be too close. The prisoner had just cracked up and couldn't take any more of it.

There were countless such instances of prisoners cracking up. One morning I went down to the refectory for breakfast and sat down beside another prisoner. To my astonishment he produced a pile of the kind of large tacks or studs you use on the soles of hobnailed boots, placed them casually on his plate and started swallowing them, one by one with his tea. Unfortunately the code among the prisoners forbade you calling out to any of the screws on duty, so we had to wait until one of them noticed something was wrong and when they did they took him away to the Mater Hospital.

Another day in Saint Patrick's we were all having our dinner when suddenly, for no reason that was apparent to me, the entire place went totally quiet, exactly like the scene in the film *Scum*, which is set in a British prison. Nobody moved, nobody said a word, but you could tell something big was about to happen from the sense of anger in the air. Suddenly, almost as if on a pre-arranged secret signal, all the tables were upended and we set about wrecking the place, smashing windows and anything else that could be broken. The screws wisely just locked the doors from the outside, thus ensuring that we were contained until our anger had subsided. Probably nothing specific triggered that riot; there was just a build-up of anger that had reached such a level it had to find an escape valve somehow.

Today there is a constant debate through the media about the effectiveness or otherwise of sending criminals to jail. All I know is that, compared to the nightmare I'd served in Daingean, and even despite the horrors I've related above, jail was a luxury. To have your own space in your own cell without anyone interfering with you was truly blissful after what I'd been through. My old feelings of loneliness had eased off too, partly because I had gradually been putting more distance between my real feelings and what I allowed my mind to dwell on. In order to cut off the pain I had taken on this false persona and effectively become somebody else through this whole period. But then, I would argue now, I had little choice if I was going to survive at all.

My mother loyally visited me in jail, probably about once a week, including through my last incarceration, in Shanganagh Castle. That final spell heralded, at the age of nineteen, the end of my sojourns in jail, although there was one more obstacle I had to surmount before I was to find myself back on the right side of the law.

Having committed yet another crime in Dublin, I took off on the boat to Liverpool. Sheila, my girlfriend at the time, whom I'd met after coming out of Daingean, came over to join me. I had by now reckoned that my only chance of any kind of a decent future was to settle down, and in order to do that I first had to convince the court that I was capable of renouncing my criminal ways.

Where I'd grown up it was assumed that if you went out with the same girl for more than two years you automatically got married, so having given it five years we became husband and wife in a registry office in Liverpool.

But on the way back on the boat to Dublin to face the court I admitted to Sheila that I thought getting married had been a mistake, that I'd only gone through with it to make myself look good before the courts and that I'd prefer if she didn't mention our marriage to her parents for a while. Understandably, she was dreadfully upset: she broke down and pleaded with me to give it a try.

In the meantime I'd begun playing music in public, and when Sheila and I came back to Dublin we lived together with her parents in Sean McDermott Street while I scraped a few shillings from gigs wherever I could find them. Her parents knew by now that we were married, but I was convinced they had little time for me and I hated living with them, so we soon had to move out of their place.

But somehow the marriage served as a kind of turning point in my life. For a start, when my case came to trial my barrister added the details of the marriage to his portrayal of my difficult family background, and he skilfully painted a picture of me as a kind of modern-day Robin Hood, robbing the rich to sustain my poor family. Even the garda who had issued the summons stood up in court and said he believed that I was a reformed character. All of this helped to persuade the judge to let me off all the charges against me.

That was my very last court appearance and from then on I went straight. Looking back on it, I don't think my career as a criminal was particularly successful anyway. I left too many clues behind me at the scene of most of my crimes and I'd been caught too easily too many times, so I obviously hadn't the proper aptitude for it as a career. I lived with Sheila for a few months before we parted, and my next visit to jail was actually to play a role in a major film, but we'll come to all that a little later!

10

THE STIRRINGS OF MUSIC

I started to get seriously interested in music around the time my criminal career was coming to an end. I won't be unduly melodramatic and pretend that it changed my life, but discovering music, especially the blues, had a major impact on me, and still has. Hardly a day goes by without me picking up either my guitar or my harmonica and having a good workout.

The stirrings of music in me had begun a long time back in my early childhood. When, during my second hospital visit, I would listen to the radio on the headphones supplied, I found I quite liked the music I heard, although, like most people at that age, I listened to music in a casual sort of way. It would never have occurred to me back then that making music could be a job from which I could earn real money.

But one of the other patients, a man suffering very badly with tuberculosis, could do little else all day except lie on his back reading a book or playing his mouth organ, tunes like 'A Pub with No Beer' and 'Whiskey in the Jar'. This small instrument captivated my imagination and I asked him to teach me to play it. Keen to help, but conscious that his medical condition meant it would not be wise for me to play any instrument he'd been using, he promised he would teach me if I got one of my own, and that's how my mother came to buy me my first mouth organ.

I used to play it all day long. Even at night I'd play it under the bedclothes, until I drove all the patients crazy with the noise I was making! It didn't take long for them to curtail my wailing by taking it away from me every night and returning it to me the next morning. My mouth organ was, in effect, put under curfew, and understandably so!

Obviously deciding that mastering the mouth organ was not enough, I took to singing for the patients as well. I sang the Cliff Richard hit 'Living Doll' in a competition I entered and was delighted to win a children's annual for my efforts. All this puzzles me, since, apart from my father playing the piano occasionally at home, there was virtually no music in my family background, but, like all youngsters, I probably liked the attention and the approval it brought. Without realising it, I think I always had a secret dream in my heart that I wanted to be a professional entertainer of one sort or another, but it only came to the surface later.

During my stay at the Irish government's pleasure in the open prison at Shanganagh Castle, where I'd been sent as part of my rehabilitation, my interest in music received another boost, although not until after I'd turned my attention to more serious educational matters. One of the few good things that came out of my stay in Daingean was that I'd studied for my Group Certificate. I was pleased to pass the exams and I continued to study in Shanganagh.

There were no bars on the windows at Shanganagh, and nothing of the heavy repressive atmosphere one normally associates with prisons, and this encouraged a more positive attitude in many of the inmates, including me, as we began to feel there might just be another, more worthwhile, way of life than crime.

At Shanganagh I figured that some form of additional education would help me if I wanted to get a decent job later on, and I was lucky to befriend a brother called Dinny from a nearby monastery who used to visit us. Dinny was a decent man, and he gave me regular free lessons in the basics of English, maths, history, poetry and so on. With his encouragement I got stuck into my books with such fervour that I would even sacrifice the attractions of watching television in order to study. Some might even say I became addicted to learning for a while, and to this day I prefer to read educational, self-help books rather than newspapers or novels.

About four months into this feverish regime of study I wandered into a room and came upon a guy playing a guitar. I was instantly captivated by what I saw and heard, and started plaguing the musician with a stream of questions – what's that for, why do you do that and so on. He very patiently explained about scales and notes and chords and even wrote out explanatory notes for me on the back of a cigarette box. I took those notes away and copied them onto a blackboard and then asked him could I borrow his guitar.

There was another guy there who played guitar and sang, and I owe a lot to him as well. I don't know what his real name was but we called him Jeweller Roe; as far as I know, he still gigs around Dublin. He virtually took over teaching me and after a few weeks I could play songs like 'The House of the Rising Sun' and 'If I Was a Carpenter'. I plagued him every few hours to retune the guitar and he always kindly obliged. I once called him off the pitch during a football match to tune it, such was my impatience.

One night when Brother Dinny walked in for our customary lesson he discovered to his great disappointment that I'd stashed all my books away. He looked with puzzlement at my squiggles on the blackboard and then he looked over at me and asked me what was going on.

'I've decided what I'm going to be for the rest of my life. I'm going to be a singer and an entertainer.'

He was stunned to hear this. 'You can't decide to be an entertainer just like that, right out of the blue,' he said.

But his protestations were to no avail. I had discovered that I had a natural affinity with the guitar, and none of my comrades believed I'd never played it before. In fact I became so proficient so quickly that the chap who owned the guitar became very jealous and actually sent his guitar home.

Undeterred, I found that there was a plastic toy guitar in the basement; on this guitar I put strings I had taken from a catgut tennis racket. I suppose that was really the first guitar I could call my own. I'd spend most of my free time practising chords with my left hand, only without actually making any noise. Another inmate, called Thomas Caffrey, told me he had a guitar at home. I pleaded with him to bring it in for me but he was too nervous in case the authorities would confiscate it, but in the face of my determined cajoling he relented and his parents brought it in for me.

I became so obsessed that I'd pretend to be sick so I could spend an entire day practising. Eventually the authorites copped on to what I was up to and they refused to feed me in order to tempt me out of the dormitory to get on with my chores!

Little did any of them know but I had discovered something of enormous value that would have a lifelong hold on me and would not only provide me with a decent living but also allow me to travel and develop self-esteem and self-confidence.

And it wasn't quite the instant decision that Brother Dinny assumed it to be. I think I'd developed a serious liking for music as far back as the early sixties, when I heard the English pop star Joe Brown, who later blossomed into a superb session guitarist, on the radio singing a song I loved about a yellow dress. I think the song was called 'That's What Love Will Do', and it was a hit for him in 1963, during the early days of Beatlemania. When I'd seen him on television I decided I wanted a big, jumbo guitar just like his, but unfortunately I could not afford one at the time.

There was a guy I knew then who owned a guitar which I coveted, but in spite of the fact that I offered him marbles, comics, toy soldiers, indeed anything I could lay my hands on legally or illegally, he refused point-blank to part with it. Even though he wasn't really interested in the guitar for himself he refused to trade it with me and I didn't get my own guitar until I saved up and bought one for £13 in a famous shop called McHugh Himself in Talbot Street when I was eighteen. It wasn't the best guitar in the world but it was a treasure for me at the time, along with my trusty mouth organ, which I had continued to play over the years.

During my brief stay in the Isle of Man I had started going to live music gigs, usually at the Palace in Douglas, and I saw the Small Faces, Cream, the New Vaudeville band and many more. I was a big fan of Steve Marriott of the Small Faces and was saddened when he died so tragically in a fire in his house only a few years ago. The Cream gig, despite the presence of the legendary Eric Clapton in the line-up and the band's superstar status, was poorly attended.

I know that many sensible people, including Brother

Dinny, quite rightly viewed the entertainment business as a risky one for any young and innocent person to pursue, but, in spite of the sharks who reportedly infest its waters, for me it was probably a far less hazardous career path than the wayward life I'd been living up to then. I'd actually been living on the edge all my life, in constant fear of one thing after another, with no let-up at all, so the uncertainties of a music career were unlikely to prove any more daunting than that to someone with my track, and criminal, record.

I've been asked whether the music I ultimately developed a real passion for – the blues – might have had a therapeutic value as well, but I don't believe that that was the primary pull. But that's not to downplay music and its part in my development. It became the central feature of my life and I've put much of my life back into my music. Many of the songs I've recorded on six different albums have been my own compositions, and they've all been autobiographical, about something or someone who has had a profound impact on me, such as 'Childhood Blues' or 'Shoeshine Man'. Some are deeply personal and emotional for me and every time I sing one of my own compositions on stage it's somewhat akin to returning to the scene of an accident. But performing music by its very nature places restrictions on the emotional aspect of your singing, and I often purposely don't get too close to the origins of particular songs because it can be too painful to do so.

In that sense singing is quite unlike acting, where,

for instance, it might be perfectly appropriate to break down, sob violently and beat the ground with your fists while screaming at the top of your voice. That might not work too well in the context of a musical performance, even if that's precisely how you feel. I have had to accept that expressing too much emotion while singing can actually get in the way of the song. An audience expects you to remain in control and stay focused. In contrast, I find acting extremely liberating and sometimes therapeutic as well, as it gives you the freedom to be less controlled and to explore and express the most extreme emotions.

I think I took to music because I'd never learned how to express or deal with emotion in anything like a constructive fashion, and music offered me an opportunity to do so without losing control. Neither had I role models in my life who could have shown me how to express my emotions, even by example.

So that interest in music was lurking under the surface all the time, long before my lengthy spell with the band The Business in the mid-eighties. It had been nurtured by the guy who played harmonica in the hospital and Jeweller Roe in Shanganagh, both chance meetings that transformed my life and provided me with the sense of purpose and the sense of direction I'd needed all my life. But it didn't solve all my problems, not by a long shot.

11

FINDING THE BLUES

When I came out of Shanganagh Castle I was determined to follow the path much-disapproved-of by Brother Dinny. A great guy called Richard Uzell propelled me further along the road. Richie, as we called him, now runs Maddens Bar in Belfast, but when our paths first crossed he was staying in Foley Street near where we were then living in Sheriff Street. I was still struggling to tune the first guitar I'd bought so I took it around to him to see if he could help me. While we were chatting he said to me, 'You like harmonica music, don't you?' So he said, 'Listen to this', and he put on an album by Sonny Terry.

Sonny was a blind folk-blues musician from North Carolina who usually played harmonica in a duo with Brownie McGee. He had this extraordinary ability to weave his harmonica-playing into his singing as if the two were virtually inseparable. But I was more astonished on first hearing this record by the very sound of his instrument.

My first reaction to Richie was, 'That's not a

harmonica that guy's playing!' He said, 'Of course it is!' I said, 'Look, I play a harmonica myself. Don't you think I know what one sounds like?'

So he patiently explained to me that what I was playing was actually a mouth organ, a somewhat different instrument to the harmonica, although to the uninitiated the names are often interchangeable (and to confuse matters even further a harmonica is often called a harp, a mouth harp or a blues harp). He showed me a real harmonica, which was only about six inches long, much shorter than my mouth organ.

So I said to him, 'Are you trying to tell me that the sound Sonny Terry gets on that record comes out of that small thing? Pull the other one!' When I realised that he was telling the truth all I could feel was a deep disappointment. I'd convinced myself I could really play the harmonica, while, unknown to me, there was a whole range of techniques and sounds, from the sound of human sobbing and crying to the power of a lonesome locomotive thundering across the open prairie, which I hadn't even touched on yet. I had to accept that I really knew little or nothing about the instrument at all.

But when I recovered from the shock my friend had sprung upon me I was more determined than ever. Little did I know it, but my musical education was merely beginning, as Richie introduced me to a succession of other musical legends, from Leadbelly to Woody Guthrie. A whole new exhilarating world was opening up to me and I was eager to plunge into it.

Whatever it was I believed I had inside me, and it was not something I could have articulated at the time, I felt I could channel it all through this magical instrument, with its electrifying possibilities. Some time shortly after these revelations began to sink in, I recall heading off with a bloke for a pint to a pub in Amiens Street and telling him as we walked along the street that I was going to become the best harmonica player in the world. So it gave me some pleasure in later years when Bono from U2, who played the harmonica himself on the band's worldwide hit 'Desire', described me as 'the best harmonica player in the world', although I wouldn't go quite that far myself!

After hearing Sonny Terry I became addicted to this extraordinarily versatile instrument. The fact that it was probably one of the cheapest instruments available, as well as one of the most portable, had made it hugely popular among poor white and black people in the USA and beyond. Like many of those people before me, I took to carrying one everywhere in my pocket, playing it night and day, with, where possible, my guitar as well. I practically slept with these instruments and became totally obsessed with them.

At the same time I fell in love with the blues. Better minds than mine have tried to explain the fascination of this beautiful music and they've all failed miserably. For me it has a basic simplicity, yet you can build limitless variations and complexities onto that basic structure. You could sit down with a blues musician you had never met before, and without any rehearsal or prior discussion he could start playing that basic twelve-bar format and after a couple of bars you could join in with him and play along as easily as you might slip into conversation.

There's an indescribable feeling in the playing and in the lyrics that reaches deep down inside you. The lyrics generally deal with real emotions and the serious matters of life, its heartaches and its thrills, death, loneliness, betrayal, abandonment and love both lost and found, and no doubt my own troubled life made me feel a kinship with the great bluesmen. I can't imagine I would have taken to that music quite so enthusiastically had I grown up in a comfortable and trouble-free middle-class home.

Soon I couldn't talk about anything else but blues music. If someone wanted to talk about any other topic, I'd move away. My life, thoughts and conversation centred around Sonny Terry, Sonny Boy Williamson, Howlin' Wolf, Big Bill Broonzy, Robert Johnson and other great blues heroes. Through the magic of their music I felt as if I almost knew these guys personally. I felt they'd experienced the same woes I'd suffered.

The blues reached parts of me other musical genres had failed to reach. It gave me a connection to the outside world and made me realise that, whatever torments and setbacks I'd suffered, I was not alone.

I remember clearly the very first album I bought. It was by Elmore James. He came from Mississippi and wrote the classic twelve-bar blues 'Dust My Broom'. When I first heard it I just thought, 'Fuckin' hell, what is this!' It truly sent shivers up my spine. His distinctive slide-guitar style was a major influence on the British blues players of the sixties, such as Peter Green of Fleetwood Mac. James's compositions have been recorded by a wide array of bluesmen, from Eric Clapton to John Mayall and Fleetwood Mac. Brian Jones of the Rolling Stones, B. B. King, Duane Allman and Jimi Hendrix were devoted fans and I was later even more amazed to hear that he had taught himself the basics of the guitar on an instrument he'd made himself from a lard can.

My discovery of this new world was, quite literally, to quote a well-known blues title, the key to the highway. After devouring Woody Guthrie's auto-biographical novel *Bound For Glory* I knew there was a great big exciting world out there I wanted to see more of. I'd seen too much of the world from the inside of prisons and cheap flats. Bound for glory myself or not, this was something I had to do, and nothing or nobody could have deflected me from my purpose then.

Becoming a musician allowed me to earn enough not just to pay my way but to travel all over Ireland and Europe, sleeping rough on floors whenever I had to, excited by the sense of freedom my new lifestyle brought me. I grew the almost obligatory long hair and beard and felt a great freedom, not knowing where I might be tomorrow and who I might meet.

But even more important, I felt I was doing something infinitely more constructive and pleasurable than robbing shops and getting into scrapes. Travel truly transformed my attitude to life and people, and gave me real hope for the future. I know it's a cliché, but travelling definitely broadened my mind. Experiencing other cultures educated me and opened my mind to previously unforeseen possibilities. Although I had mitched a lot from school I had still managed to learn the basics of reading and writing, so I was able to add to my knowledge through my travels.

Since I have never attended formal classes in music, I would generally be regarded as a self-taught musician, but I have learned enormously from countless other musicians I've met on the road down the years, including the aforementioned Richie and a guy called John Meehan who lived in Liberty House and taught me a lot about the guitar.

Johnny Norris, whom I regard as one of the best Delta-blues guitarists in Europe, was another major influence, especially in finger-picking styles. I went on the road with Johnny, playing all over Germany for seven months solid, as well as to Holland, Austria, and France and elsewhere, including many places I had previously visited alone as a busker.

In the early days I performed only songs written and recorded by other musicians. It had never occurred to me that I might be capable of writing my own compositions and expressing personal views and feelings in songs of my own. Then one day I received an unexpected phone-call from a researcher on *The Late Late Show* on RTÉ television. They were putting together a programme about controversial plans to build a road through part of Dublin's inner city, which would result in people losing homes they'd lived in all their lives and being moved to unfamiliar surroundings to live among strangers. The researcher asked me if I would consider writing a suitable song specifically for the forthcoming programme. The pay-off was that I'd get to sing it on the show, which had a huge nationwide audience, so I readily agreed.

I could easily identify with the people about to be dispersed from an area of Dublin in which they, and probably their parents and grandparents, had lived all their lives. The attitude of the city planners, typically indifferent to the dislocation their plans would have on human lives, angered me. So I poured my thoughts into my first original composition, 'Dublin's Inner City'. The reaction to it was so positive that it was released as a single by a group called The Jolly Beggermen and reached number two in the Irish charts. It astonished me that the first song I'd written had become a hit.

In my subsequent recording career I've been fortunate enough to release half a dozen albums featuring many of my own autobiographical compositions, such as 'Childhood Blues', 'Louise Baby' – about my daughter – 'Religion', 'Been Alone Too Long', 'Lost Lover' and 'Running Man', but I'll always be grateful to *The Late*

Late Show for providing me with the impetus to discover a talent that had remained dormant until then.

But despite all the acclaim and success, I continued to suffer, and still do to a lesser extent, from fairly low self-esteem. I still regard myself as a very shy man by nature, with little confidence. I'm never very likely to push myself the way others might push themselves without feeling the need to apologise.

In my music I've always striven towards expressing a sense of truth. I've tried in my singing to be as true to my own voice as I can. Critics and fans alike have noted that, unlike many other British and Irish blues singers, I don't adopt a fake American drawl when I sing the blues. When I write songs the lyrics deal with my real life and my own experiences, feelings and thoughts. I avoid falling into the 'Well, I'm going to Chicago' school of blues songwriting which you hear from some people even though they have absolutely no intention of going to Chicago and wouldn't be able to find the place on the map!

I have actually visited Chicago but was very disappointed with the live music on offer in what has been described as the home of the blues. I went to six or seven clubs every night but they were full of blokes with fancy shirts, medallions and all the fake shapes. While doing the rounds there I met the legendary Buddy Guy from Louisiana, who had taught himself to play with a home-made guitar when he was in his teens. He was with his wife, but he had only one thing on his mind – how to find really mild cigarettes in America like the ones I was smoking. I told him all he had to do was buy normal cigarettes and put pinholes in the tips. People often suspect that when blues musicians get together we discuss the finer points of the music, but now you know. I also saw Johnny Winter play a great gig at the Limelight.

But my disappointing visit to Chicago at least inspired me to write a song called 'Shoeshine Man'. I stopped on the street to ask this shoeshine guy would he polish my leather harmonica-holder. He agreed and then asked if he could have a blow. He turned out to be a more genuine blues exponent than the people I'd seen in the clubs, and he shone my shoes for free, so I wrote that song for George.

Contrary to most people's assumptions that I should be interested in every facet of the music and even keen to trace its routes back to its places of origin, I've never had much inclination to go trawling for old bluesmen around the Mississippi Delta and poking my nose into their lives. For me the blues is a music that is not confined to one area. It touches all of us in some way in our lives, no matter what our race, colour or creed. Without a doubt, the white man can sing the blues, and the white woman too, and you never have to go far to look for it. I can even hear the blues in the voices of Irish traditional singers. I hear it in the music of players like J. J. Cale, Doc Watson, Jesse Fuller and Tony Joe White or in the superb harmonica-playing on the

Canned Heat record 'On the Road Again', and that's by a white guy, the late Bob 'The Bear' Hite, who was a Californian.

Despite the success I've enjoyed and the years of stage experience I've amassed, I find the business of public performance a constant struggle. I suspect that at times I go out there on stage before an audience hoping for yet another dose of reassurance that I have some worth as a person. After all, playing music in public requires some kind of courage, and every time you play music, even for one individual, you risk rejection. I see it on the one hand as a means of expression and a means of communication, and on the other as a search for approval. Whatever success I appear to have achieved has never really touched me and I feel that to some extent I act a part all the time, as if what happens to Don Baker the musician 'out there' on that concert platform has nothing to do with the Don Baker here inside me.

Initially people think I'm quite self-confident, but those who know me only a little will tell you how shy I really am. When I have to meet somebody I haven't met before, or if I have to do something I'm anxious about, I get very nervous about it and have to psych myself up to go through with it.

If I go into a room full of people, I'm the one most likely to seek out a corner to hide in. I'll turn my back on the throng and will probably be the first to leave. I don't feel good enough – it's as simple as that. Unfortunately, some might put it down to a kind of stuck-up attitude, but the reverse is the reality.

Of course, being a public performer has helped me enormously to deal with some of my problems of self-esteem, but it doesn't really change my true inner feelings. Part of me has always felt different and inferior, even if mentally I know I'm not inferior.

So when it comes right down to it, I still suffer from, to borrow the title of a song on my album *Almost Illegal*, 'The Same Old Blues'. I guess I always will, and I may never know precisely why, although I've made it my life's work to find out.

12

SONGS AND STORIES

I suppose to the outsider most of what happens to a professional musician seems as if it's the result of thoughtful and careful planning. Of course, sometimes that's exactly how it happens, and it would be a foolhardy musician who thought he'd get very far without some degree of forethought and planning, but more often than people realise, unexpected and unforeseen circumstances can determine the outcome of many matters.

To give an example from my own musical career, take the title of my first album, *Almost Illegal*. It's perfectly understandable that some people who were familiar with my past thought I was making some kind of ironic reference in that title to my prison escapades, or implying that the type of music I played was so way out and anti-establishment that it was nearly illegal, but the truth is somewhat different and a lot more bizarre.

Few people know this, but when you an artist intends to release an album the recording is rarely done straight off. Instead, it usually takes shape through several stages. Initially you do a few demos of the songs under consideration and maybe some test recordings with some of the musicians you hope to use. You might try out this studio and that producer before making final decisions. Then you start working out some kind of final track listing and you could then go into a recording studio to lay down some backing tracks, which you might intend to take to another studio to be added to and have vocals and other stuff added on.

Because the recording process can often be very intense, requiring long stretches of deep concentration, and you might feel a little self-conscious about things that don't work as well as you'd like, you usually want as few distractions as possible. As a result, most artists prefer not to have too many guests in the studio while recording is in progress.

But now it was time to start the recording of my very first album, a very important moment in any performer's career. So we booked time in a Dublin studio which was very impressively kitted out with state-of-the-art equipment. I was also delighted that both Brian Downey, who used to play drums with Thin Lizzy, and John Kearns, who'd played with Stockton's Wing and Mary Coughlan, had agreed to play drums and bass guitar on the session.

Initially, matters proceeded more or less as expected, while we were in the process of laying down some backing tracks. Then suddenly we were interrupted by some uninvited and unknown guests who looked like serious customers indeed, and I didn't think they'd dropped in just to order copies of my album, for some reason. Little did we know it, but the now-defunct studio was about to become defunct before our very eyes, even as we were attempting to work on the recordings! Unknown to us, the studio owed considerable sums of money to several creditors, and our unexpected studio guests were actually bailiffs who had come to take away whatever was of value in the studio in lieu of money due.

Of course the other musicians, the engineer, the producer and I all explained to them that we were in the middle of a very important recording, and we begged them to give us another couple of hours. But our pleas made little impact and in desperation we pleaded for just five minutes to do another take of the song we were working on. This worked only up to a point, and matters took a really absurd turn when I was actually in the middle of recording another take while one of the burly bailiffs was demanding that I give him the very chair I was sitting on.

I jocularly remarked that it was almost as if we were doing something illegal, even though we were simply making a record, and the phrase 'almost illegal' immediately seemed to make the perfect title for the album. So that's really how my first album got its title and I'm sorry if the truth behind the title spoils the very inventive theories that some critics came up with.

In a sense the same spontaneity comes into play with regard to my own instrumental development and musical compositions. When I work on my harmonica-playing I often deliberately try to imitate different sounds, not just the obvious ones, like trains and birds calling, but some sound I've just heard, like some object hitting the floor, a door slamming, the screech of a distant car braking, a car wheel splashing through water – anything to challenge my limitations.

In relation to the art of songwriting, I know there are many songwriters who have a very disciplined approach to their craft. They might have a set-up in a small room in their house, which they treat nearly like an office, and every day they go into that office and work at their songs. I'm not knocking that approach; I know it works for some, but it's not for me.

It's a common misconception that songs arrive with the composer complete, exactly as they appear on the record, when in reality they are more often than not pieced together bit by bit, maybe over a period of months, or even years. Usually for me a song starts with something that simply appears spontaneously, maybe while I'm driving in my car or doodling with my guitar or harmonica. Mostly I write sitting down with my guitar, which I play every single day unless prevented by practical circumstances. I'm not necessarily consciously trying to write songs all the time but sometimes they emerge when you least expect them.

There are no rules and regulations about writing songs. A composition might start with a short catchy riff, a snatch of a melody or a vague feeling or an emotion or a memory I want to express in music. It might be a few words that have some importance to me and make me want to expand on them in song form. Sometimes I might feel there's something there I want to express but I don't know what it is and I struggle to reach for it and turn it into music. Of course you have to be open for when such inspiration comes along, and you often have to work to see if the inspiration is there. If that inspiration provides you with a mere scrap of an idea you may then have to work at it for a while to turn in into a usable piece. One thing you can bet on – songs rarely write themselves.

That working-out process can take months, and you have to be careful that in your haste to complete a song you don't force it and thereby spoil it. In time I think you develop an intuition for what you know will work, so there may be a line or two in the lyrics that doesn't quite sit properly and you may spend some time looking for a better phrase or word. Sometimes you reach a point where you have to admit that the song is not really going anywhere and you just have to forget it. Too many songwriters are totally convinced that everything they write is good, but that's rarely the case. Yes, it can be frustrating to reach that point where you have to admit that the song you might have put a lot of work into is never going to work. You have to become self-critical and honest enough and have the artistic conviction to give in and admit it's failed. That's what waste-paper baskets are for! Then again, I might be playing around with a piece this week before realising that it fits perfectly with another unfinished scrap I had been working on last year, as if some subconscious creative process was working on the song all along, unknown to me.

I'll regularly jot down bits of lyrics if I think I'll want to use them, and when I think a song is shaping up I'll record it on a cassette machine at home to see how it works and what changes it might need. Very occasionally a song emerges almost complete, with melody, words, a catchy chorus and all the other components one after the other, in quick succession. I think songs like these often make the best songs.

And so the struggle for artistic expression goes on. I might have a complete song written but with nonsensical words, which I'll then tackle and tidy up. I think every creative person must find the way that works best for them.

For me, lyrics are an extremely important aspect of every song. I want to sing songs that reflect real feelings and that are about real life, not inane fantasies. That's no less important a consideration even when it comes to choosing to do cover versions of songs by other songwriters. I've little time for lyrics of the 'I can't live without you' or 'I'm gonna love you 'til the end of time' or 'We've gotta get ourselves together' variety. These sentiments are rarely, if ever, taken from real life or real conversations. They're simply clichés picked up from other songs. They reduce songwriting to mere painting by numbers, and the end result more often not is songs that merely produce a harmless sound while communicating nothing of substance.

For one song of mine, 'Lord Have Mercy', which I released on the *Born with the Blues* album, the lyrics flowed out in one great surge and almost complete. After a little experimentation I fitted those lyrics to two separate musical ideas I'd already worked on some time previously, so in reality you could argue that it's actually three songs in one, yet I think it all hangs together quite organically.

For another song of mine, called 'Driving', which I included on my solo album *Just Don Baker*, I got the initial spark of inspiration while driving in my car when I noticed that the constant thrum of the windshield wipers might make a neat bass line. So I went home, took out my guitar, worked out a riff and built a song around it. It gives me great satisfaction when a song like that turns out really well and fulfils the initial artistic impulse behind it. 'Running from Freedom' is one song with which I've always been very happy and 'Been Alone Too Long' is another of my compositions which I think really worked out the way I wanted it to.

Unfortunately that's not always the case. Some years ago I wrote a song called 'I Can't Take No More'. I think I was looking for a specific reggae feel in the recording and I don't think we caught it, especially in the drumming. I don't mean that the drumming was technically wrong. Perhaps I wasn't able to communicate to the drummer exactly what I wanted, or maybe I didn't quite have it right in my own mind. All I know is that it didn't work the way I wanted it to, and that's always disappointing. Unfortunately, when a song has been recorded and I'm unhappy with it, it can cast a dark cloud over that song, to the extent that I can't listen to the recording with any pleasure. Whenever I think of the song I can't help recalling my intense dissatisfaction with it.

Then again, maybe one day I'll find that elusive vibe and record it again, and all will be well. On the other hand, I know there are lots of people who actually like that particular recording, but they're hearing it from the other side, so to speak, and I can't hear it with the fresh, unbiased ear that an outsider can bring to it.

Virtually every one of my songs is deeply personal and autobiographical. I think that explains why I've never been attracted to the prospect of collaborating with other songwriters. I'm aware of various collaborations between different writers, like the recent work by Elvis Costello and Burt Bacharach, for instance, and I have to admit that sometimes it can work. But I think it can at times be a very contrived way of composing and the contrivance can often be obvious in the unconvincing nature of the end product. Maybe I'd learn something from working with another songwriter, but until I feel inspired to work with someone else I'll give it a miss.

Of course the songs rarely end with the writer,

anyway. With me, the next stage is usually to bring it to the band I'm working with at the time and see how it works with them. Things can go wrong. The groove I've worked out for the song might get lost in a band situation or maybe some of the other musicians might not feel that same groove or I might not be able to convey exactly how I want the song to feel. It's easy to get the notes right, but getting the right feel or the right emotional intensity can be much more elusive.

Quite often that experience of transposing the song from a solo work to a band item can bring a whole new dimension to a song and you have to be open-minded enough to allow for positive input that adds something to your song. When it works, I don't thing band musicians are given sufficient credit for the creative role they play in putting a final shape to a writer's work. The songwriter gets the credit and the royalties, but who knows, maybe the record only sold because of that really clever fill the drummer dropped in after the third verse or the classy counterpoint melody the lead guitarist worked out.

So at every stage the song can change and grow and you can find new aspects to it all along the way. Sometimes in the process of working out a band arrangement you realise that the song needs an extra line or the chorus needs to be shorter or whatever, so you take it back home, 'back to the factory', as we say, for adjustment.

A famous songwriter, I think it might have been

Sting, once said that songs are never really finished. Instead they are abandoned at the point when the writer feels that he or she has nothing more to add to them. I tend to agree with that notion, but I also feel that it's important that the writer knows when to stop. I've heard many potentially good songs ruined because the composer kept adding one more verse, or repeated the chorus too often or made the intro too long. As with much else, when it comes to songs there is much truth in the axiom that less is often more.

Just as a song in the hands of a solo musician is different from the same song in a band context, so too there is a vast difference between playing live and recording. Personally I don't like recording. I like the response you get from a live audience and the tension it brings to the music, so I prefer to do as much recording as I can live in the studio, since I don't have the patience for the tedium of forty takes and spending two days to get the bass-drum sound right.

I've also learned that just because a piece works in a live situation it doesn't mean it'll work as well on record. In the modern recording studio you don't have the interaction between the musician and the audience, for a start, and your actual audience may be restricted to the engineer and the producer, and that factor can alter the way you feel the music as you play it. Musicians have used all kinds of tricks to overcome this, including drugs, but to little or no avail.

I also believe that too much emphasis on the

technical aspect of recording can make the music sterile, and that's fatal in blues music or any music where a level of emotional intensity is essential. I find slower songs tend to work best in the studio, perhaps because the energy of a live gig is more crucial for an uptempo song, but I've heard great songs totally lose their spark through an insensitive approach to recording them.

Then again, the reverse can happen. I recorded a tune called 'Dallas Rag' on *Just Don Baker*, and I still have to practise that to make it work as well live as it did on the record. But this kind of thing is a rarer occurrence.

Other differences come into play depending on the line-up of the band you use. Sometimes a song works with twelve musicians and sometimes one or two is all it needs. I've enjoyed playing with all sizes of bands, but the solo experience is one where you perhaps have the best and worst of everything.

On the one hand, the solo musician has total control over the music. From a performing point of view he can, on the spur of the moment, decide to finish a song there and then or repeat a couple of verses if he feels like it. It's much harder to be that spontaneous with a band, for obvious, practical reasons. Playing solo you don't have a drummer to keep time for you, and there's no second guitarist to decorate your work and for you to play off. I tend to get more nervous before a solo gig, and nervousness with musicians tends to result in two things – you play louder and you play faster – and neither is helpful to the performance. But when a solo gig works, you and you alone get all the credit.

With a band you have other people with whom you can share the responsibility if things don't go down as well as you expected. A fair amount of blues music is improvised around standard patterns, and by its nature improvisation brings the risk of mistakes here or there. The blame for the bad fuck-ups can be blurred, too, and you can hide in a band if you've had a dodgy gig yourself. In fact I often hide behind the microphone on stage if I'm not comfortable. It gives me a sense of protection from the audience – not that I need it in a physical sense, but it serves as a kind of psychological protective barrier.

It can also be fun to have others along with you to share the joy of a good gig or a challenging piece of music that worked the way it was intended. Fortunately the latter has for me been the more common of the two in recent times. When it works and you know the crowd have got something from it too there's no feeling like it in the world.

Long may it continue.

13

Angry Young Man

John Lydon, formerly more familiar to us as the spite-fuelled Johnny Rotten of the Sex Pistols, has a song in which he sings that 'anger is an energy'. But some of us believe that all anger is automatically bad and should be permanently avoided if at all possible. To me anger is a healthy emotion if you express it while it's 'white'. But if you let it go to 'red' without letting it out, not only are you risking serious problems for yourself but those close to you might also be in danger. The English writer Thomas de Quincey wrote that 'Man should forget his anger before he lies down to sleep.' In fact, I prefer to think that instead of forgetting it he should deal with it, and preferably long before bed.

Many of us have been conditioned by society in general and by our families, friends, colleagues, bosses and educators in particular, to believe that it is preferable to suppress our anger rather than risking being offensive or hurtful to others, and so we allow it to build up inside us until something trivial may send us over the top. When that happens it usually looks to the outside world as if we're losing our temper over nothing much at all, thus further adding to the unease for everybody involved. But few understand how a long-festering wound that hasn't been dealt with properly, or a succession of perceived slights that have accumulated inside us, will inevitably lead to the pressure building up to the point where it needs release. In my case I used alcohol for years as a means of 'eliminating' my anger. I thought that if I didn't feel anger then it must have gone away, it must have been dealt with somehow.

Unfortunately, there are too many social conventions that prevent us from expressing our anger as soon as we first feel it. Some of these conventions are understandable: for example, we may not wish to introduce unpleasantness into a situation or a relationship, so we'll avoid expressing our true feelings. We may be fearful in the face of some disagreeable aspect of reality, or we may simply hope that the anger will pass unspoken and unnoticed. Sadly, it may not pass at all and may continue eating away at us inside for who knows how long, causing immeasurable damage.

I've eventually had to learn to deal with the fact that I've felt anger, an intense anger, for as far back as I can remember. I'm still struggling to deal with it every day of my life. But I had to learn the hard way that alcohol never provides the answer and only makes matters worse in the vast majority of cases, mine included.

Killing that cat when I was young, for example, that came from my uncontrollable anger. Drinking was my misguided attempt to cover up the anger, but it often only led me into fighting constantly with guys and losing my temper for apparently trivial reasons. I remember fooling about with a chap until the zip of his jacket accidentally hit my throat and really hurt me. That simple incident set off an explosion of anger and I grabbed a hurley stick and laid into him. He fended me off with his arms until my aggression subsided, but my anger was so intense I could probably have killed him. My violent reaction was totally out of proportion to the mild pain I had suffered.

I carried this anger everywhere I went and into every relationship, platonic or sexual. After about six years in Corporation Buildings my family, including parents and all five kids, had moved about a three-minute walk away to a three-roomed flat in a terrace, Common Street near Sheriff Street, in houses not dissimilar to those portrayed in *Coronation Street* on television. But no matter where I moved, my problems moved in with me, and the environment, and my reaction to it, were no less vicious in the new area around the new address.

Of course I had friends, but most of them were from the same deprived background and in the same social situation as I was, with criminal records and experiences of living on the edge all the time, so there was little chance of anyone taking me aside and convincing me to change my ways or face my reality. I had no identification with anyone outside that social grouping and no clear understanding that there might be another way of life.

I've heard it said many times, including once by a film critic discussing the underlying motives in Alfred Hitchcock's film *Psycho*, that all the problems between men and their mothers are about sex. That, as I was later to learn, albeit reluctantly, could be the nub of all my own personal traumas, traumas often resulting in the expression of my darker, inner side in a frenzy of horrible rage.

I was often, I must admit, violent towards women too. A violent fit could be brought on by unjustifiable jealousy, in turn provoking that old fear of abandonment again. If I found a close female friend paying attention to another man, no matter how innocently, all the feelings concerning my mother and her lover would come back to me again and again, followed by wave after wave of hostile anger. While Sheila and I were going through one of those silly phases where a relationship is all off one day and all on the next, my inner violence erupted uncontrollably against both her and Benny, a male friend of hers, one night during a row in Burke's Pub in Moore Street.

I occasionally used to play gigs there, sometimes with Richard Uzell, in return for free drink. Any time I thought of Benny hanging around Sheila when I wasn't with her, a rabid jealousy would began to boil up inside me, even though deep down I knew they were really just friends, nothing more than that. He might have asked her for a date a few times, but I don't think she ever responded in a way that would have encouraged his overtures. Unfortunately, in my state of mind the truth was usually irrelevant.

That night I'd stopped off on the way down to the gig in Burke's to buy a new switchblade knife, not for violent use as it happens, but because I needed one for the more innocent task of tightening the screws on my harmonica. Just around closing time, as I was returning to my place in the pub after visiting the toilet, I spotted Benny standing close to Sheila – too close, as far as I was concerned. I immediately saw red, took out the brand-new knife, flicked it open and lunged towards him in a mad rage. Sheila screamed when she saw me heading towards them with my eyes blazing, and Benny jumped back with fright and tried to grab my hand. I sliced his hand open with the knife, but Sheila also tried to grab the knife away from me and in the fracas I stabbed her hand too.

I can still remember Benny trying to get the door of the pub open (it had been closed to stop any more people getting in), with blood pouring out of his wound, while other people in the pub were throwing chairs back in order to get out of my way. I then took another run at Benny, fully intending to thrust my knife into his back. Luckily, the barman, a chap called Vinny, jumped over the counter, grabbed me by the shoulders and prevented the knife plunging into Benny's back more than a half-inch or so.

That barman may have saved Benny's life and probably saved me from a lengthy prison sentence.

Fortunately the inner city code at the time was that you tried to sort out such personal problems among yourselves without 'squealing' to the cops. But I still feel remorse to this day over my inexcusable violent actions, but I later learned in therapy that it wasn't Benny I was trying to kill, but, more than likely, my mother's lover.

I always lived on the edge then, permanently risking somebody doing me in and inflicting serious damage on me, but the rage inside me wouldn't allow me to duck any kind of trouble, no matter what risk there might be to life or limb. Like most people I knew in that neighbourhood of Dublin, I fought with hatchets, blades and whatever else came to hand. I usually carried a blade of some sort hidden in my sleeve and I was always ready to use it.

My relentless anger made me blind to fear and often foolhardy. Very late one night I fought three burly dockers with a hatchet and actually skulled one of them. I was drunk again and joyriding around on a motorbike somebody else had stolen. Its broken exhaust was waking the kids in the neighbourhood and understandably annoying the other residents. One of the dockers threw a rock at me as I sped past them and it hit my knee.

Quickly dismounting, I furiously raced up to a nearby flat and demanded that the woman living there loan me her hatchet. She knew I was up to no good and tried to shut the door, but I burst in and took the hatchet I spotted over by her fireplace.

Back on the street I hid the weapon behind my back as I approached the three guys, angrily demanding to know, 'Which of you hit me with that rock?' One of them calmly said, 'I fuckin' did, so what?' so I leapt at him and cracked him on the head with the hatchet, causing blood to spurt out all over his face. The other two backed off very quickly and I went home, satisfied that I'd put them in their place. This was just one of numerous examples of my violent flare-ups, and my rages were not confined to males getting too close, as I imagined, to my female friends.

Around the time of my late teens I used to hang around with Tony, the barber whom I'd seen viciously stabbed in prison. We'd first become friends in Marlboro House and had later linked up again in Saint Patrick's Institution, and we'd kept up our friendship when both of us were back on the outside.

But even with Tony I feared abandonment or rejection, especially if a third party entered the picture, and even if the third party was male. There was nothing remotely homosexual in this, but I'd come to rely a lot on Tony. At least he understood what I'd been through and we supported one another. When a chap called Billy came on the scene and started drinking with us, without realising it or knowing what was going on inside me I became very insecure about him being around us and very jealous of him as a possible threat who might come between me and Tony.

In the pub one Monday night, without any provocation and in a deliberate attempt to aggravate Billy, I threw a lighted cigarette into his pint. A huge brawl ensued, tables and chairs were thrown and we were all ejected from the pub. As we left, Billy said he was going to get me.

The following morning I was walking down to collect my dole when he appeared out of nowhere and ran towards me, brandishing a knife. I quickly took off my denim jacket, wrapped it around my arm for protection from his swipes with the knife and managed to get away from him. But the culture of that environment at that time was such that a serious conflict could not be left unresolved, so I knew there was more of this to come. In anticipation of further attacks I got a chef's two-pronged fork, which is normally bent, and straightened it out with a hammer so that I could hide it up my sleeve in such a way as to be able to remove it quickly whenever the need might arise.

Nearly a week passed, during which I was regularly intimidated by some of Billy's gang members. On the following weekend I was standing outside the local chip shop when Billy came out of the shop. When our eyes met he angrily said, 'What the fuck are you looking at, Baker?' to which I replied venomously, 'You, you stupid fucker.'

As soon as I'd said that he ran towards me with his knife again, but this time I was better prepared than on the previous occasion. Reaching for my own weapon I quickly withdrew it from my sleeve and slashed his finger down the side, while he did the same to me, before I sidestepped him and plunged the fork into his head. He fell on his knees and then down on his face, blood pouring all over the pavement. Neighbours and onlookers were running around screaming, while part of me actually wanted to go in for the kill. Instead I walked away, back to the family flat in Common Street near Sheriff Street, washed the blood from my own cut finger, and bandaged it.

Then came a knock on our door and when I opened it I was confronted by Sean, Billy's best mate, who was clearly out to avenge his pal's defeat. Knowing there was trouble in the air, my father blocked me from going out, but I pushed him out of the way, chased Sean down the stairs and smashed a bottle over his head.

Fortunately for both of us, that bottle was empty, as a full bottle could have killed him. I then began to beat the shite out of him. A crowd had gathered around us again and when I had finished with Sean I yelled, 'Anyone else want to take me on?' But nobody else did and that was the end of that particular violent episode.

There is no question in my mind now that this incident was entirely my fault, sparked by my insecurity and needless jealousy, and it's not a part of my life of which I'm particularly proud. Only later did I even stop to consider that I must have been an appalling person to be around. Was this tendency towards violence a kind of cultivated bravado or was it a way of disguising my fear? Or was my inner rage towards my mother, my father and the whole set of circumstances I'd lived through overriding my fear? Maybe I'll never know.

Either way, a little of that fear, violence and anger dissipated after I started playing the guitar and really getting into music. I can't quite explain why or how, but I reached a point where I think I allowed myself to feel a little bit of that fear and accept it for what it was. Certainly, other people felt that my harmonica-playing expressed much of the anger that frequently welled up inside me. I remember coming off stage after playing a gig one night, and Christy Moore, who'd been watching and listening from the side of the stage, said to me, 'Don, what are you so angry about?' In all innocence I said, 'Me, Christy? Angry? What are you talking about?'

'For fuck sake,' Christy says, 'You were stamping the stage so hard when you were keeping the beat that I thought you were going to put your foot right through those floorboards!'

Christy could see, not only from the aggression of my playing but by the way I was violently keeping time stamping my foot, that I was a troubled soul. He could see something I could not.

In one of his books Pat Ingoldsby has a poem which he wrote about me. It's called 'For Don' and you'll find it in Pat's collection *Salty Water*. It's about me being on stage and the side of me the audience sees, but there's one line where he says, 'They didn't see you in your dressing room.' That line refers to him being in a dressing room with me before a gig when he saw me putting on my harmonica belt; this probably reminded him of the actions of a gunslinger in a western movie. He told me he knew what I really wanted to be strapping on, and he was right.

14

THE BUSINESS OF MUSIC

When I was becoming more proficient in my music, and a bit more confident in my own abilities, I played a lot around Dublin with various musicians and busked all over the Continent, spending a lot of time in Holland and Germany especially. So I reckon I've been a serious, professional musician in one way or another since I was about nineteen.

There were long stretches of time when I would wake up in the mornings and play guitar and harmonica virtually all through the day until I went to bed again that night. Even when I was eating my lunch or dinner I would often continue doodling on the guitar, working on some part of my technique or trying to polish this riff or that run. At one point I even dabbled with the mandolin and the banjo in the belief that proficiency on either instrument might bring me some gigs on the Irish folk scene.

This infatuation with music drove anyone who lived with me at the time to distraction, but the stuff I learned through such dogged dedication has been a great asset to me in my music career.

I remember the very first time I heard myself on tape. We had a casual music session one night in somebody's house and I was vaguely conscious that there was a tape recorder of some sort there. A few weeks later I called into the house of a friend called Jackie Brennan and he played a home-made tape of a guy playing a harmonica. I was quite impressed with what I heard and was even more delighted to hear it was me!

My first television performance was also an event I still recall quite fondly. I was gigging in Toner's Pub in Dublin's Baggot Street when the late Aine O'Connor, who was presenting a programme called *Summer House* on RTÉ at the time, saw me and invited me onto her show.

For my small-screen debut I was joined by guitarist David Naughton, with whom I busked regularly around Dublin and overseas. We did a blues song called 'Candy Man': this is not to be confused with the hit by Roy Orbison but is a song I'd learned from the Reverend Gary Davis from South Carolina. I was so in awe of the cameras that I spent the entire performance staring at the ground, with my long hair falling down to conceal my face.

Such nationwide publicity lead to an increase in the level of gigging and it was actually on the way home from one of my many live gigs in Dublin that I happened to save three lives. It was Christmas Eve and a kind female fan with her own car had agreed to drop me home with my instruments. But just as I was about to lock my door her car came screeching back towards my door, her urgency made even more dramatic by the fact that a large cardboard box had become lodged underneath her chassis. She jumped out in an obvious panic, shouting at the top of her voice, 'There's a house on fire just around the corner!' Quickly locking my instruments securely inside the house, I jumped in beside her and she drove us around to the scene of the fire, the Railway Bar in nearby Oriel Street. I could immediately see smoke and flames billowing out of the windows. Steel shutters were on the front doors and when we pulled up I could hear screams from an upper window.

Although my driving experience had mostly been confined to stolen cars I urged my friend to let me take over the wheel. Narrowly missing a lamp post I manoeuvred the car up onto the footpath and as close to the wall as I could manage. I then jumped up onto the car roof, then up onto the window ledge and kicked the glass in, tearing my leg to shreds in the process.

There were three frightened people inside, Thomas Doyle, the pub owner, his wife, Maria, and their babe-in-arms, all virtually naked. I first helped their baby down and then the other two and drove them around to the nearest hospital. Convinced that they were in safe hands, I was about to set off for home when Thomas asked me to go back to look after the pub until the police arrived to check things out.

Back at the bar it wasn't long before the fire brigade

arrived. They broke down the steel shutters with sledgehammers and hosed the place down and soon had the fire under control.

Next day Thomas called to express his thanks and took me around to his pub for a few drinks on the house. It was ironic, in view of my drinking problems and the fact that on Christmas Day it is traditionally impossible to find a pub open anywhere in Ireland, that here I was with a pub full of free booze and a grateful owner at my disposal.

Equally unfortunately, because of the day that was in it there were no newspapers to record the heroic deeds of yours truly, so I had even more reason to enjoy Thomas's largesse. He more than repaid his debt later. When I badly needed a break he offered me a job as a barman in the very same pub.

Of course my growing drinking habit, combined with my increasing profile and popularity, had made me somewhat arrogant as well, and I expected the moguls from the music industry to beat a path to my door, so I didn't bother to look for a record deal or a publishing deal. Sooner or later, I reckoned, they'd realise that the record industry wouldn't survive without me and they'd form an orderly queue, brandishing blank cheques, outside my door. For some unfathomable reason, this has never happened!

But through the hard grind of playing and doing any television shows that came my way, my reputation, especially as a harmonica player, grew and I was invited to put together a tutor book called *The Harmonica*. That brought me in some useful money and gave me increased status as a musician. The publicity also helped increase my public profile, and more gigs came in.

Bono's public description of me as 'the greatest harmonica player in the world' came as an extra boost to my profile too. I first learned about his comment when I got a phone call from my friend Michael Collins, who was living in the USA, to tell me what Bono had said during a live gig. I think it was in San Diego, during a major U2 tour when the band was enjoying massive popularity worldwide.

Of course I appreciated Bono saying it, but I'm realistic enough to be aware of the dangers of allowing yourself to think like that, so I prefer not to dwell too long on the implications of his accolade. Somebody else somewhere probably thinks I'm the worst harmonica player in the world! Actually, I met Bono after a private screening of *In the Name of the Father* several years later and he walked over to me, put his arm around me and said, 'Sorry about that!' as if he was fully aware of the burden he'd inadvertently placed upon me by his generous comment. I was also seriously flattered when my harmonica-playing hero Charlie McCoy recorded an instrumental of mine called 'Jordana', named in honour of my only daughter with Jo.

After I published my second tutor book I was invited to adjudicate a major worldwide harmonica competition in Jersey in the Channel Islands. On the one hand I was flattered by the honour of being invited to sit on what was a very illustrious panel of judges from the USA and Europe, including the brilliant Madcat Routh, whom I much admired. But at same time I was anxious about being in the company of so many acknowledged masters of the art and having to live up to the accolades.

The adjudication part of the event was most enjoyable, although I have some reservations about musicians judging other musicians in those competitive situations. But later, when I saw Madcat performing, I was so stunned by his artistry that I became even more nervous about having to perform in front of an audience comprising so many harmonica aces. But there was no way out.

Then I bumped into a classically trained group and asked them if they'd back me, and, after I had explained to them the basics of the twelve-bar blues pattern, they agreed. So my gig started and in the middle of the opening tune I stopped them and told them I'd have to sack them. One of them instantly responded by saying, 'But we were playing on time!' To which I retorted, 'But you weren't playing *in* time', and the audience erupted with laughter and that broke the ice for me. I was quite happy with my performance after that and I got a standing ovation! That was probably the most satisfying compliment I was ever paid as a musician, getting that response from my international peers.

On the morning after that gig, unable to sleep and still elated by the reception I'd received the previous night, I went for a walk along the pier near the hotel and met up with Madcat, who asked me could he meet me later so I could show him some of my techniques. To have had such a request from someone I admired and respected so much is something I will treasure always.

But in a sense Madcat posed a problem for me, as I have never been able to explain or analyse what I do on the harmonica. Whatever way I play, it is a purely personal and instinctive style, and as soon as I try to break it down into component parts I lose track of it and it all falls apart. So while I'm happy to be told that I have a unique approach to the harmonica, I'm afraid I can't explain what it is or how I developed it.

I tried to analyse it once, but after making a list of some of the characteristics of my playing, the way I shake my hand and so on, the effort brought on heart palpitations and I vowed never to do it again. Unfortunately, some regard this as evasiveness on my part, as if I'm selfishly refusing to share some invaluable secret, but the truth is that I simply don't know how I do it. I suppose it's like riding a bicycle – as soon as you start asking yourself how you do it you fall off.

As for what I might have done with my life had I not found music, I've given this considerable thought over the years and I suspect I'd either have been institutionalised or be long dead. I can't imagine any other pursuit captivating me as wholeheartedly as music did.

Maybe music brought me the only kind of relationships someone with my emotional problems is capable of sustaining. I've always enjoyed an instinctively positive relationship with musicians, especially fine Irish musicians like Jerry Hendricks, with whom I've played guitar for over fifteen years, as if we shared an invisible bond and had a mutual respect.

I've met some decent music-business people and some despicable ones, so to that extent I presume it's no different from any other business. Wherever the spoils are high you'll find corruption, and some people can be only too eager to cheat at the expense of others. We've seen this become an increasing problem throughout the sporting world both in Ireland and internationally, so it would be silly to expect the music business to be any different.

It wasn't until I'd given up drinking that I became much more serious about my music and began to treat it as a career. In time I made quite a lot of money, out of which, unfortunately, the taxman and the VATman both took large chunks.

Some of my emotional problems have also adversely affected my musical endeavours from time to time. The old sense of anxiety would often come on me just before a gig. I remember gigs at the Universal Folk Club in Parnell Square when I used to almost literally rattle with fear before I'd go on stage, but I was by then convinced that if I kept facing that fear I'd eventually overcome it. Most musicians suffer some nerves before a performance, and I still do, but my attacks back then were in a league of their own and, for all I know, that anxiety might have injected an extra frisson into my performances.

15

ON THE ROAD

For a musician, going on the road is like entering a strange world far different from that experienced by anyone living a 'normal' life. Going on the road means being away from home, missing loved ones and familiar surroundings, often for long periods at a time. It sometimes means the claustrophobic, confined world of a tour, where every day is governed by the need to get to the next gig, surrounded by the same musicians and crew and perhaps travelling in cramped conditions in less than complete luxury. On the other hand it can be the most liberating notion in the world, setting out with the total freedom to take any turn in the road that pleases you, opening yourself to new cultures, new people and new experiences.

On the road you are often at the mercy of people you might meet under the strangest of circumstances, so trust in humanity is a must. You often find yourself in places you didn't know existed, merely because you decided to take a lift from that person or the offer of a floor to lie on from another. I've been on the road in one form or another on both sides of the Atlantic for over twenty-five years and my travels have certainly taken me into some strange places and odd situations. I've met some oddballs too, but I'm sure that for others there were times when I fitted into that category myself.

For a while I took up residence in the town of Heidelberg in the southern part of what was then West Germany. I busked nearly every evening in the Uniplatz, the University Square, which was very popular with students and with American soldiers from the nearby army base. I was quite popular too, with my trendy beard and long hair, and I found it to be quite a lucrative pitch, although it had other side benefits.

For instance, there was a bistro at one end of the square where they would regularly change my coins into notes for me, and the owner would present me with a complimentary schnapps for every song I sang. Needless to say this often had a questionable effect on my behaviour. One night, no doubt with one-too-many schnapps on board, I clambered onto a parked Volks-wagen to sing. When the owner came back he waited politely to give me the chance to get down, but when he saw I had no plans to comply with his wishes he simply drove off, down through the streets of Heidelberg with me on the roof singing the blues to the astonished pedestrians! Fortunately he good-naturedly kept his speed down to about ten miles per hour so I was in little danger, but eventually he stopped and ordered me off. Of course such escapades added to my notoriety in the area and I was ultimately sorry to leave, but the lure of the open road inevitably proved too tempting to resist.

When that siren-call came it arrived in a most unusual guise. One night after a busking session I was approached by a freaky English guy with a Clint Eastwood-style cape who began to tell me how much he liked my music. I must have hinted that I was thinking of moving on, because he then invited me to meet him in his bus at the railway station for breakfast next morning to discuss the possibility of our travelling on together.

On the basis that I had nothing to lose, next morning I set off to the railway station. When he told me he had a bus I assumed this was a euphemism for something no bigger than a Hiace van, but the only bus in sight at the station was a large touring bus with English registration plates and the destination 'Blackpool' emblazoned on the front.

After scouring the area in case there was some other vehicle that might be his, I eventually decided to try him at this one. I knocked on the door and he arrived to greet me wearing nothing but a pair of jockey shorts. When he showed me in I was astounded. He had converted this bus into excellent living quarters, with curtains on the windows, most of the seats removed so as to leave plenty of space for bunk beds, a wash-hand basin, plus a superb music system and other mod cons.

He argued that if we teamed up he could provide

the transport to take us anywhere we chose to go and out of the money I earned busking I would pay for his petrol and give him something towards his food, which, he claimed, wouldn't be much because he was a vegetarian. This was too much to resist, so I bade farewell to the good burghers of Heidelberg and travelled all over Germany and France in this strange living room on wheels.

So this Englishman and I made a good pair. He, as I quickly discovered, was an acid head and I was an alcoholic, even if I didn't yet know it. We picked up a moped somewhere so that, maybe on account of parking restrictions in a particular town, or for sheer convenience, we would often simply park the bus on the outskirts of a town and use the moped to transport ourselves and my guitars into the centre.

I reckon I must have been the only busker in the world with his own tour bus! But sometimes I'd have to wait a few days in the same place for John to come down from one of his countless acid trips. He'd be sitting somewhere for hours on end in his cross-legged yogi pose while I played my guitar or experimented with the local drink. But it was all part of the freedom of a life that was in sharp contrast with my upbringing and my incarcerations in various institutions.

Not all of the fun and games took place overseas. I remember playing in a band called Firehose Reel with the actor Brendan Gleeson, who's a tremendously humorous bloke. The hardest thing about being in a band with Brendan is trying to keep a straight face. During one gig in Ireland he started to tell the audience this extraordinary story about a bunch of American troops who were torpedoed in their ship and were lucky to make it alive to a nearby island. The story got more and more bizarre as it went on until it ended with Brendan saying 'and that that's how one of the blokes came to write our next number, "Black Mountain Rag".' This was a very fine explanation of the background to the song except for one minor detail – the story was a complete load of nonsense Brendan had made up on the spot!

Life on the road is not an endless routine of carefree capers. The nature of the musician's life creates an environment where drinking can very easily become a central part of the daily routine, simply because there's too much time to kill and so few other options. It can hardly be a coincidence that so many musicians, especially those in the Irish trad and folk fields, have had serious problems with alcohol. Fortunately, most of the people of this type that I know have courageously won their battles and have bravely talked openly about their problems. They include many artists who are household names in Ireland, such as Frances Black and Mary Coughlan. Nor is this a problem that afflicts exclusively Irish musicians. A whole pantheon of international rock stars, from Eric Clapton to the late Keith Moon, have struggled, with varying degrees of success, with the same demons.

If you've never been a working musician gigging around a country you will have no idea how easy it is to slip into drinking as a way of life. If, for example, you are booked for a gig in a small Irish town far from Dublin you might arrive in that town quite early in the day. You might have an interview with the local radio station as early as ten o'clock in the morning to help promote the gig taking place later that night.

Next you might meet somebody from a local newspaper for another interview and eventually visit the venue to check that all is in order regarding sound, lights and all of the other paraphernalia that go into putting on a gig. But even if you do a very comprehensive sound check there are still hours and hours to kill before you hit the stage at nine o'clock or later in the evening.

Quite often the only place of social interest is the local pub, which may serve as the only available meeting place for friends or business contacts. Because of the social aspect of music itself, most people, including the fans who make you the success you are, often expect you to enjoy a drink with them. Not to comply can inadvertently give offence and may often be misconstrued as stand-offishness.

So operating in the music world obviously brings with it the standard temptations which are not just confined to the road. The phrase 'sex and drugs and rock 'n' roll' sadly describes graphically what that life can be like. Although I drank alcohol until I was often barely able to function as a musician, I was never tempted to get into other drugs. I tried hash a few times but although I've been a lifelong smoker, I didn't take to it at all, and it actually gave me palpitations. I tried LSD too but, for whatever reason, nothing at all happened, so I never took to that either, and that's as far as my experimentation went. I was probably offered every drug imaginable at one time or another, but I've had no difficulty turning them down – except alcohol, of course – not through some amazing strength of character, but because of either indifference or fear or both.

Even the sight of a needle has scared me from the time I was in hospital, so any drug that had to be injected was not for me anyway. In that respect I was lucky. Alcohol was a drug I was familiar with from its common use by my father and in the society around me, so I assumed I knew the limit of the risk and its effects.

So today, whenever I go out on tour, I generally like to have a fairly full diary. I arrange to meet old friends, and if I'm in a foreign country, check out the local music scene. I never go on the road without a selection of books and I find I get more work done that way without damaging my health. But I still prepare for the unexpected, without which going on the road would be less of the exciting adventure it invariably is. Besides, how else can you cure itchy feet?

16

AMONGST WOMEN

I had my first girlfriend, as far as I can remember, when I was about thirteen. Her name was Mary Esther, and such was the terror I struck into the parents of any girl who took up with me that in order to discourage her from hanging around with me her father shaved off her hair.

That was the only serious relationship I had with a woman until I met Sheila, my first real love and the woman I married in Liverpool after my spell in Daingean. But Sheila left me after we had a heated argument – only one of many – in a pub, and we went our separate ways for about two years while she moved across to London to live with her sister.

In the mid-seventies I had settled into a serious relationship with a girl called Elizabeth. All was going reasonably smoothly until Sheila reappeared out of the blue and she and I spent some time together in a flat I had in George's Street. Sheila convinced me that I needed to make a concerted effort to make our marriage work and argued that I hadn't really given it a fair shot.

So she returned to London, hoping I would follow her to resume our marriage where it had left off.

After some hesitation, I left Elizabeth behind me in Dublin in a very distraught state and convinced I was totally crazy to be rejoining Sheila in London, getting a job on a building site to earn some money. But after two weeks with Sheila I realised I was missing Elizabeth badly and I had to accept once and for all that, even with the best efforts on both sides, our marriage was never going to work satisfactorily. I wrote to Elizabeth sharing my new-found doubts and she wrote back asking me to come home, saying that all was forgiven and that we'd be okay together. Unfortunately Sheila must have had her suspicions by then. She found the letter and read it, so when I came home from work one evening my bags were literally packed and ready for me.

That night I had to resort to sleeping in a bathtub on a building site. The next day was Friday and when I got my pay packet I decided to toss a coin to decide where I would go next. If it came up heads I'd go to Holland, for no apparent reason other than that it was comparatively easy to get to from London, but if it landed tails I'd go back to Ireland.

That coin landed tails, and that flip of a coin signalled the end of me and Sheila. I was happily reunited with Elizabeth in Dublin and she was shortly to become pregnant with my eldest daughter, Louise. Meanwhile Sheila was now pregnant in London with my first child, our son Glen, a situation that I learned of after she informed my mother about it in a letter. I didn't doubt her claim that I was the father, as she was not the type of woman to indulge in any kind of deceit. In fact when I look at our son Glen, now in his mid-twenties, he looks like a clone of Don Baker.

Although the marriage to Sheila lasted five years, for much of that time we were hardly ever together. Apart from my regular jail visits and my gigging up and down the country, we were constantly fighting and drinking in what was in reality a rerun of my parents' marriage. I don't want to blame my parents, but it's been said that 'What you live with, you learn, what you learn, you practise and what you practise, you become.' In my case this pithy saying seems to be totally accurate. Because of what I'd witnessed throughout my own upbringing, I assumed that the way I lived my life was the same as the way everybody else lived theirs.

I didn't meet my oldest son, Glen, until he was about five years old, and even then it was by chance. I had a very pleasant part-time job, looking after kids, taking them swimming, to the pictures or the park. I was in a Dublin cinema one day with a group of them when he recognised me. I'd been on television performing as a musician several times by then and people had told him, 'That's your da on the telly!'

So when he spotted me that day in the cinema he just casually walked up to me and said, 'Hey, you're my da!' It was as weird, simple and unexpected as that, although it was also quite traumatic for me. I'm actually very fond of kids and I loved him instantly; I later asked a social worker to ask Sheila if she'd let me see him once a week. But because I was drinking heavily at the time they agreed to my request only on the condition that I promised to meet him on the same day every week. Unfortunately, when our regular meetings began I'd often take him into pubs with me and sometimes keep him there with me all day long. Later he told me how much he used to hate being in the pubs in those days. But I'm really very proud of him now. He works today as a professional musician in Tenerife and he's never been in trouble with drink, drugs or the police.

Not surprisingly, in due course Elizabeth, or Liz, as I called her, left me too, after one drinking session too many, when Louise was about one year old. More than a decade was to pass before I saw my daughter again. I wrote the song 'Louise Baby' for her one morning in Germany after a sleepless night when I couldn't even drink myself into oblivion. She has latterly studied psychology as part of her ambition to work with the police, so both she and Glen have made extraordinary lives for themselves, especially given the poor example I set them. During my battles with the forces of the law I certainly would not have considered it possible that a daughter of mine would join the police!

People have naturally asked me whether I ever considered that I was putting my son and daughter through exactly what my father had put me through, but I can honestly say it never occurred to me to see it

Don Baker's gang, O'Connell St, 1966.
From left: Don, Joxer, Gollier, Shannon, Fagan, Giller.

Don aged 19 in 1969, singing for £2 a night
in the Maid of Erin pub, Marlborough St, Dublin.

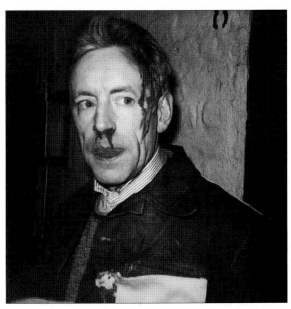

As Joe McAndrew in *In the Name of the Father*,
after the row.

A BBC TV appearance, 1990.

At Salthill Festival, 1992.

Alone in the spotlight in the Olympia, Dublin, 1993.

World Harmonica Championship in Germany, 1992.

Concert for Aer Rianta, Dublin Airport, 1995.

Courtesy Pat Baker

Courtesy Pat Baker

Courtesy Cathal Dawson

in that light. Later, both of them told me quite blatantly they hated me for what I was doing, not just to them, but to myself, drinking and frittering away every pound I earned.

It may not have been too obvious to people, but I had made periodic attempts to curb my drinking. When I was about twenty-seven and living with a girl called Áine, who worked for a newspaper in Dublin, I made a serious and sustained effort to quit drink, although I still had no suspicion that I might be an alcoholic. Nor was it ever mentioned by any of the doctors I attended for various ailments. They just gave me tablets, from very large duck-egg tablets to Valium and who knows what else. For a time I was on tablets to help me sleep, tablets to help me eat, tablets for just about every normal human function. If any of them provided me with any relief, it was temporary.

When I was off the drink, even for a short while, the horrible feelings of loneliness would invade my mind all over again, and the fretting and mistrust any time a woman went away from me, even for the most normal and innocent of reasons, returned. Looking back, it seems as if the drink was serving as a makeshift dam to hold in my real feelings.

When I stopped drinking I replaced my addiction to drinking with an addiction to Áine. After a few days without alcohol I would become totally obsessive about her. I wanted to know where she was every second of every day, what she was doing, who she was with and so forth. If I heard she'd gone somewhere with somebody else I'd telephone that place and find out what time she arrived and who she was with. If she'd left I'd want to know at what time she'd gone and with whom she had left. All in a blinding panic and totally irrational, but born of my intense fear of being abandoned again as I had been by my mother all those years ago in the hospital.

Needless to say, Áine soon tired of this constant harassment, as anyone would. She felt suffocated by my obsessive desire to control every part of her life, and we parted.

This was part of a common pattern in my relationships with women. If a woman rejects my efforts to control her then I cannot help but become very fearful. In common with others who have addictions, I have tried at times to control everything around me: I could trust nobody, and that need for control itself often became another addiction. That desire to manipulate is, I now suspect, a manifestation of my deep-seated lack of trust in women. In due course I had to learn that this lack of trust was my problem, instead of transferring the responsibilty for it onto all the women I'd been involved with, but that learning was way ahead in the future.

Perhaps my desire for such unreasonable control in part explains why I attacked Sheila's friend Benny with that knife, and why I couldn't bear to risk Billy coming between Tony and me. It may also explain why I've never had what I'd call a close circle of intimate 'mates', nobody I could share my deepest thoughts with, outside my relationships with women and the musicians I've played with in one band or another.

I don't think I can come up with any explanation other than my need to control everything raising its head time and time again. If it's my band, I can exercise some control over the musicians in some way or other. If it's a male-female relationship I must try to control that too. As a result, most of my relationships have ended with people leaving me.

While I'd been off the drink during my time with Áine I'd made some serious efforts to build my health back up again, and I took to running ten, fifteen, twenty miles every day around the streets and parks of Dublin, in what became yet another obsession! But it was shortly after that that I met Jo, who was to become my second wife, and she's still my closest friend even though we've been separated for years now.

There are a few others whom I'm proud to call my friends, but they're very few in number and I'm not sure if I can ever let them get too close to me. I can control my life better when I'm on my own. Besides, when I'm not feeling the old anxieties I can be quite happy and contented with my own company.

17

You're in the Army Now!

Not many people know this, as a certain well-known English actor would say, but I spent some time in the Irish army. In many ways, my spell with them came about by accident and as a result of my impulsiveness, but my entry and exit from the army were no less memorable for all that.

It all began when my father came to me one evening and tried to persuade me to give up playing about with this blues music, which he regarded as a complete waste of time, and to get a proper job with some long-term prospects, security and steady income.

Like many a father before him he saw little future in the blues. 'If you were playing some decent Irish ballads like Ronnie Drew and The Dubliners, you might at least be able to go down to the pub and earn a few shillings,' he jibed at me, before adding, 'If you had a real job, even if it was just sweeping the streets, at least I could be proud of you.'

I thought this was a bit rich coming from a man who'd practically drunk his own family into starvation, but his words obviously stuck in my mind. A short while later I was coming home from a gig for which I'd received no reward apart from the customary free drinks, when I bumped into two chaps I knew; they told me of their plans to join the Irish Army the next day.

Without even thinking about it, I asked them to call for me on their way so I could to enlist with them. It was as simple as that. Since the army band was famous throughout the country I had quickly worked out that here was a brilliant opportunity for me to develop my musical career. I would join the army band, learn to play the saxophone, get paid for it and live happily ever after!

On arrival at Collins Barracks on the South Circular Road I asked the recruiting sergeant whether, if I completed all the training, I would be able to join the army band. He said I would, and the photograph I saw in his recruitment office with a soldier in full uniform playing the bagpipes reassured me that I was on the right road at last.

I served the first nine months in Cathal Brugha Barracks in Rathmines, a healthy walk from our flat in the centre of Dublin. Later I did a spell in Collins Barracks, and from there I moved to McKee Barracks on Blackhorse Avenue. I suppose my stint in the army wasn't too bad, considering I only joined on a whim and because I had thought the army would turn me into a proper musician, but it was not without its difficulties.

The first few days were sheer bloody torture – long hours of hard physical exercises of a kind I'd never imagined. Each night would see me back in my bunk with aches and pains everywhere and trembling from the day's exertions. I think they used this tough baptism to sort out those who had 'the right stuff' from those who simply were not cut out for such a rigorous life. But it brought out the stubbornness in me and, in what was almost an exact replay of the way I learned to deal with my difficulties in Daingean, I soon resolved that the Irish Army was not going to get the better of Don Baker.

When I had completed my first nine months' training I went to my commanding officer and explained to him that my ambition was to join the Army School of Music and commit myself wholeheartedly to it. When he told me it was a twelve-year commitment I was so enthusiastic I said it should actually be twenty years. Then he asked me how old I was. I think I was either twenty-three or twenty-four at the time, and I told him.

Then he dropped the big bombshell. 'You're too old to join the army music school now, I'm afraid. You really should have come to us when you were about seventeen.' Thus abruptly ended my career as an army musician, but since I was already enjoying life in the army for the most part I carried on, despite this blow.

In spite of my previous unhappy experiences with a variety of authority figures, I had settled down to army life quite comfortably and found it to be very much like a family, perhaps a surrogate for the family I'd never had, with a great comradeship among the men. Sure, we were ordered around by our superior officers, but it was all done within established boundaries. I knew the score and accepted it without argument or reservation. When the officers were off duty they behaved like normal, decent blokes and you knew they had a difficult job to do, with a lot of responsibility for a body of men and a lot of expensive and potentially dangerous equipment and weaponry.

I could also see that my colleagues were going through the same regime as me, and each of us was treated equally. Not that I'd left all of my old troubles outside the barracks door. Whenever one of my close comrades was about to leave or move on as part of his work, I'd suffer considerable anxiety, sparked off yet again by the fear of abandonment.

It was during my spell in the army that I had a very serious panic attack, after which I ended up in hospital. It occurred over one of my weekends off, when I used to play a gig in a small pub. I was walking nonchalantly past the Ambassador Cinema at the top of O'Connell Street with my guitar on my way to the gig when panic suddenly hit me with such force that I simply fell to my knees and let out a piercing scream.

I don't know for how long I stayed on the pavement, but eventually I staggered back to my feet. My legs had turned to jelly as never before and I could barely find enough strength to walk, but eventually I struggled into a nearby pub, where I sat down and tried to recover.

One of the barman quickly spotted there was something seriously wrong with me, but, as usual, I couldn't properly explain how the attack made me feel. Sometimes it felt like I might be going crazy, so I could never admit the full impact of these incidents to anybody for fear that I'd end up in an asylum.

The kindly barman made a phone call and I was taken by ambulance to a nearby hospital. The doctor on duty asked me all kinds of questions as to whether I was using LSD or any other drugs, which I wasn't, but he didn't ask me anything about my drinking habits, which I later thought very strange. After his inter-rogation he gave me a very strong dose of Valium – ten milligrams – but told me I could leave as soon as I felt up to it. I lay on a bed for a while and then went straight to a pub, where I downed about ten pints in an attempt to feel normal again.

The odd thing about such panic attacks was that the effects would disappear as quickly as they had appeared, and by the following day I would be back on duty as if nothing had happened. But then one day I got a shock of a different sort, one for which I was even less prepared and which you may find hard to credit.

The current international political situation, espe-cially in the Middle East and parts of Africa, gave rise to much speculation as to where any one of us might be posted, which foreign army or band of guerrillas had the most awesome reputation and how we would all dispatch them with heroic deeds and great valour. But I had never bothered to think seriously about this matter up to then and it came as quite a surprise to realise in my naivety that the Irish army was not really all about comradeship and keeping fit, or playing music, for that matter. Instead I might find myself in situations where I could expect to be shot at, and, even worse, would be expected to shoot back and kill people!

Of course I knew that armies trained for war, but other countries went to war, not Ireland! In my original desire to see the army as a mere musical training ground, I had conveniently overlooked the fact that since the sixties Ireland had built a fine reputation for its contributions to United Nations peacekeeping forces in trouble spots as far away as the Congo in Africa, where brave Irish soldiers had been killed in the line of duty. You might imagine that a man of my violent history would have been perfectly suited to life on the front line of battle, perhaps even eager to get stuck in without undue delay, but I believe my reluctance proved I was not a naturally violent man. My commitment to the army was further affected by the death of my father, whose prompting had led me into the army in the first place, and my now-deflated army-related musical ambitions.

Matters finally came to a head when the Irish republican activist Sean Mac Stiofáin was confined to the Mater Hospital during a period when the troubles in the North were in serious danger of spilling over into the South. The killing of innocent Irish people by the British Army in Derry on Bloody Sunday in 1972 had aroused understandable anger among many people throughout the island. Mac Stiofáin was being guarded by members of the Irish Army and there were protests outside the hospital by Republican sympathisers. These protests were getting so ugly that there was likely to be some blood spilt.

It then came to my attention that some of my neighbours and friends were among the demonstrators; the prospect of Private Don Baker in full riot gear, shield and baton having to club his unarmed and defenceless mates was one which did not appeal to me in the slightest. So I took the only reasonable course of action I thought was open to me. I disappeared over the wall of the barracks and went AWOL (absent without official leave).

In order to disguise myself over the coming days I grew a beard and let my hair grow long, but eventually the police called to our house when I was present and I was taken into custody. After being transferred back into army custody I was brought before a tribunal and ordered to be confined to barracks with a list of duties that included polishing floors and stuff like that. I managed to put up with that regime for just about a day and then I legged it over the wall, AWOL again.

I knew this couldn't go on indefinitely, so some time later I checked myself into the army hospital at St

Bricin's near the Phoenix Park, where I exaggerated my worries and anxieties as much as I could and told them that my anxiety attacks were so bad that I was taking drugs and was in danger of becoming an addict. I tried to convince them that I was the last person in the world who should be trusted with weapons that could terminate people's lives. The ruse worked a treat, and without further delay I was given a full medical discharge.

From that day on, the world's trouble spots have had to sort themselves out without the help of Private Baker D. In all, I served two years and a couple of months in the army, won my third star and had reached a level of physical fitness that I believe stands to me to this day. And most importantly, I didn't have to beat up my friends.

18

THE ROAD TO RECOVERY

After my relationships with Sheila and Liz I was the father of a son and a daughter by two different mothers. In fact Glen and Louise were born within six months of each other, although they didn't meet until they were in their mid-teens. It was daunting for me to have the responsibility of telling them they were brother and sister, but they took to each other instantly and have been great mates ever since. But that came later.

The divorce from Sheila left me free to marry Jo, whom I'd met at the Holyrood Hotel in Harcourt Street after a gig. She says she saw me through the gap in a bar through to where the gig was taking place and her instant reaction was 'There's the guy I'm going to marry!' Later, when she told her parents that she'd nearly fallen off her chair with that shock of realisation, they told her it was a pity she hadn't!

At this point I was no longer using tablets. I was feeling quite fit, relieved to be able to sleep and eat without artificial aids, and I felt fairly confident that I finally had my drinking under control. But professionals believe that you should avoid making a serious life decision until you've stopped drinking for at least two years and given your head time to clear and adjust to normality. Deciding at that point to undertake such a serious step as another marriage was pure folly on my part.

As my mother had since passed away, Jo and I moved into her flat in Ballybough. At first it seemed as if we'd known each other for years, and we got on very well together. Before long she gave birth to my third child, a daughter we called Jordana.

But after a relatively short period of genuine contentment and happiness my renewed drinking began to become an emotional and financial drain on both of us and a dark cloud hung permanently over what had been a promising future. I was earning steady money as a musician, but I was drinking it away as soon as I got it and doing the same with any money I could scrounge from Jo, who was working full-time as an industrial engineer. Alcoholics become very good liars, and I'm not sure if I ever allowed her to realise the full extent of my drinking in the early days.

In truth, my drinking had become so bad that there were many days when my first priority, from the second I woke up, was to find alcohol. As I described at the beginning of this book, it would not be long before Jo, like Liz, Louise's mother, reached the end of her patience with me. I was rarely there for her or Jordana, and she was particularly concerned that, despite her best endeavours, my drinking was destroying any purpose I had in life and was in danger of affecting the welfare of baby Jordana.

She'd helplessly watch me undergo a negative personality change whenever I was drunk, suddenly turning from being manically ecstatic into being deeply depressed and full of anger, at the other end of the spectrum. I'd become sullen, withdrawn and argumentative over the most trivial matter. I'd be critical and sulky when she was around, but if others joined our company I'd switch back to my bright-and-breezy self again. Today Jo feels I behaved this way with her and not with others because I felt safer with her, whereas the others might not let me away with it so easily. She may be right.

Despite my many bouts of anger I'd never been violent with her and never hurt her physically, although I threw things at her now and then in my raging fits. But I know I came close to going over the top on several occasions, including once getting her up against the wall and threatening her with a nail file placed right up against her throat. Understandably, she was truly frightened of what I might do either to her or to Jordana when I got into one of my regular drink-fuelled angry moods.

Jo threatened to leave me several times but hadn't followed through on it, and perhaps that lulled me into a false assumption that she would never leave me. Then a time arrived when I had to face the fact that she meant it and that she intended to take Jordana away from me too. She'd gone through phases of not allowing me to look after Jordana at all because if I got drunk I might forget to feed her or to take proper care of her. Sometimes she'd walk in the wind and rain with Jordana in the pram all the way to her mother's house so her own mother could take care of our baby, thereby allowing Jo to go to work, because she couldn't trust me or because I was away gigging or, more likely, away somewhere else in my head.

Eventually she broke down in her office one day, and her understanding boss, who had a son with similar problems to mine, advised her that if she really loved me she had no real option but to leave me. On her way home in a taxi to our house she actually had second thoughts but she arrived at the house to hear Jordana crying and me, who had been left to mind her, nowhere to be seen.

To make matters worse, she had no key and was unable to help our distraught daughter. She even tried to break the windows to get in but failed to do so. In panic and rage, she tracked me down to the pub, where I trotted out the usual feeble excuses, but to no avail this time. She'd had enough and I was now about to lose my wife and the daughter with whom I'd just begun to develop a relationship.

Jo assumed that alcohol was the primary source of our marital problems, including my infidelity. Meanwhile I was beginning to wonder if I was destined to spend my whole life with women leaving me on account of my drinking. Deep down I think I was finally beginning to suspect that alcohol might be a bigger problem in my life than I had been prepared to admit. But I was a long way from acknowledging just how serious my situation was and my initial course of action was quite a devious one. In order to prevent Jo from carrying out her threat and moving out permanently with Jordana, and to pacify her in the short term, I agreed to go along with anything she suggested. After one night away from me, spent in her sister's house with Jordana, she came home and I was convinced I'd won her back. What I failed to realise was that Jo had probably left me emotionally a long time back.

Although it would have been the most sensible step, I didn't commit myself to giving up drinking once and for all. That was a sacrifice I was not mature or honest enough to make for a long time yet.

At Jo's insistence I started to attend the rehabilitation centre in Stanhope Street, located between the Smithfield area of Dublin and the North Circular Road. Of course she did not suspect that my attendance there was merely a cheap ploy to win her back and keep my daughter. Unfortunately, in some respects, the ploy had actually worked, and unknown to her I had already worked out the next stage in my deceit. I would keep off the drink for only as long as it took to see her happy again and until the dust settled on our domestic relationship. I knew I was due to play a gig in Monaghan in three months' time and I had worked out exactly how and where I was going to get the drink I still craved.

After you register at Stanhope Street they give you an assessment based on a questionnaire which enables them to tell you whether you have an alcoholic problem or not. Their first major task is usually to convince you that you do have a problem and that the problem is an illness rather than some moral failing on your part.

Jo herself, by now pregnant with our second child, Jackson, began to attend Alanon, an organisation for spouses of alcoholics, a step she initially resented, because she believed that I was the one with the problem, not her. Later she admitted that while she was not addicted to alcohol she might have been addicted to me or to our relationship, and that realisation gave her a fresh perspective on our situation.

During an early bout of therapy I recall that something sparked Jo into screaming out, 'I'm not your mother! Stop blaming me for all this!' I was a long way from recognising the part my mother played in my alcoholism; Jo must have worked out that connection long before I made it.

The counsellors tried to make me accept that my life had become unmanageable because of my drinking. I was encouraged to take my first substantial step towards dealing with my problem when I was handed a sheet which had printed on it, 'I, Don, have a problem.' As with the others in the group, I was expected to copy out this admission in my own hand and accept what it said.

While everybody in my group openly recognised their problem and admitted it, I would write that maybe I drank a little too much, and maybe this, or perhaps that, all to avoid the admission I urgently needed to make if I was ever to deal properly with my difficulties. They made me do this writing exercise several times, but each time I refused to go the whole way and admit the source of my problem. I simply couldn't bring myself to write what I was supposed to write. I was in denial and didn't dare face it. But they persisted and after numerous attempts I finally made the admission that would start the process of my rehabilitation.

While the others in attendance had connected with their feelings, I hadn't been able to do so, and, what's worse, didn't realise that I had failed to do so. It's that connection with the root of your problem that brings on the pain and it's only through experiencing that pain that you can deal with the cause of the emotional problems that are being assuaged by your dependence on drink. I finally and with enormous difficulty admitted that I had a serious problem, but little did I know that the work to heal myself was really only beginning and that it would be a long, tortuous road to recovery.

The counsellors worked steadily and methodically on me over a couple of months before I was finally forced to admit the inadmissible, that since alcohol was causing problems in my life, I was by definition an alcoholic. But, metaphorically speaking, I had to be dragged kicking and screaming until that reality hit me like a lightning bolt. After three months in Stanhope Street the penny had finally dropped.

This came as a profound shock to me and catapulted me headlong into a deep, prolonged depression. Was I so like my father before me after all? Had I learned nothing from what he had done to his family?

Yes, I was an alcoholic and I had to accept that the only solution for my illness could be nothing less than the complete renunciation of alcohol forever. Having the odd drink for social reasons would no longer be an option; it had to be a total break or it would not work. Unfortunately, alcoholism is not an illness that somebody else can cure for you by simply giving you a tablet or booking you in for an operation.

At the beginning they'd been giving me Valium but eventually they said that had to stop too as they insisted on my being completely free of all drugs. This healing path was a journey which I had to face on my own and head-on. There would be no more sly evasions, no more paltry excuses, no more empty promises, no more putting off the inevitable. I would get help and support from others, but there was really nothing they could do for me unless I took control of the situation myself.

Inside, I think I'd already begun to suspect there might indeed be another way out of my mess, a way of living without being stuck in the past to the point of being condemned to keep repeating it and re-experiencing it ad nauseam. The time had come for me to grow past all that, no matter how painful it might be.

And it was painful. The effects of withdrawing from alcohol dependence have been very well documented over the years, so I won't go over the same details here. But immediately after I stopped drinking I went through what they call the 'honeymoon' period before the shit kicked in and all hell broke loose in every part of my being. Nothing quite prepares you for the awful sweats, the uncontrollable shakes, the vomiting nearly every single morning and the fact that your thoughts are perpetually dominated by the fear of what the future might hold for you. I had the most agonising anxiety attacks and horrific nightmares. I can still see the maggots I imagined crawling out from the pit of my stomach. This agony went on uninterrupted for a full year and all through this torment I kept thinking that all I needed was one drink, just one small drink, and then everything would be okay. But deep down I knew it wouldn't be.

Contrary to common assumption, knowing that many others were suffering just like me, perhaps for reasons similar to mine, did little to alleviate my situation. In the end you have to deal with this as your own personal problem, and the number of other fellow sufferers and their proximity, sympathy and willingness to help are no real consolation.

I attended Stanhope Street for six months, three nights each week. I remember them asking me to write down three things I didn't like about myself. In a matter of seconds I had the answers. Then they asked me to write down three things I liked about myself. This totally baffled me. My self-esteem was so low I could not think of a single thing I liked about myself, not one, no matter how long they left me there to come up with an answer.

I've since learned, although with some difficulty, to accept that there are things about Don Baker that I actually like. But that took a long time coming too, not because I underwent a dramatic personality change, but because I simply learned to face the truth in myself with honesty and because I'd grown to accept myself as a human being with the myriad fallibilities and virtues that such acceptance entails.

Learning about co-dependency was another breakthrough both for me and Jo, and I was relieved to know that there were sound explanations for my bizarre behaviour patterns. As a result I became a little more at ease with myself and easier to live with as the guilt receded slightly. It is sometimes impossible to convince an alcoholic that their illness is not their fault in a moral sense but is instead caused by some fault in their metabolism.

The writer Mark Frankland wrote about his own mother's alcoholism and referred to the shame associated with it. He described her as 'too obstinately conventional to let anyone absolve her from the shame of drinking, and I wonder now if she clung to her shame because it was a last piece of the identity she was losing. She could not stop drinking, but at least she could hate herself for it.' Having been through it myself, I can see exactly what he's getting at, and it takes a while to shake off that shame.

Recovery for me was to be a slow, gradual process, partly because you can seldom really see the results of the work you're doing on yourself. You're battling on more or less in the dark, with no clear picture as to where this journey is leading you. You just know in the depths of your being that you have to travel that particular lonely road; there's no other option.

In time, and with Jo's help and indefatigable energy, I started to deal with my problems, and my confidence started to come back little by little. At the start I did gigs in a venue in Capel Street, where at first even playing to ten people was a struggle, but it seemed to be getting easier and better as time went on.

I thought I was cured. But I was wrong.

19

More Pain

Two whole years off the drink and I felt worse than I had ever felt in my whole life, with frequent anxiety attacks and poor-quality sleep. I was also not eating properly and was feeling very uptight and stressed. Worst of all, without alcohol there was nowhere to hide from my pain. I was still extremely angry and I would lie awake through the night feeling this extraordinary anger and hurt. Sometimes I assumed it was all part of the recovery process, but at other times I suspected there was something more fundamentally wrong with me. But what might that be?

So in desperation I went back to the people at Stanhope Street and explained the extent of this fairly recent development to them. One of the counsellors suggested to me that I might have to look back to my life before I had begun drinking at all in order to discover what had driven me to take to alcohol so heavily in the first place.

This was a blow to me, not least because it was totally unexpected. I had only recently accepted, with great reluctance and much pain, that I was an alcoholic, but now there was the suggestion of greater, more deep-seated problems somewhere in my past. Were my previous thoughts of madness true after all?

Dealing with the primary cause of my anger was to be particularly hard because I had put so much self-protective distance between my real inner feelings and the person I was outwardly trying to portray on a day-to-day basis. It was probably fair to say that I didn't really know anything about my true self, who I was or what I felt about anything. Drinking had long ago buried the causes of my anger deeper within me, to the extent that reaching the true original causes had become an even more complex undertaking.

I had become truly scared of my anger because I was dumping on everyone that came my way, sometimes in the most unreasonable fashion. On my way to an Alcoholics Anonymous meeting one evening I stopped at a small grocery shop to buy an apple. The incident made such an impression on me that I can remember that the apple was 35p and I paid with a 50p coin. Just as the man serving behind the counter was about to give me my change a woman cut in to ask him a simple question. Instead of continuing to deal with me he started to reply to her query. I instantly exploded with rage and threw the apple viciously at him, shouted a few expletives and stormed out.

I was like that all the time. I became so impatient that I couldn't wait for a bus without getting angry and aggressive. When a beggar innocently asked me for 10p on the street one day I grabbed him and pinned him against the wall and thought I was actually going to kill him.

I would wake up, on those few occasions when I would manage to get to sleep, and it would seem as if there was someone sitting on my chest, such was the physical and mental pressure I'd feel. I had become a walking anger machine and I was scared that some day I would really go too far. So I decided to attend the Rutland Centre to see if they could help me deal with this frightening anger.

When I arrived there the female facilitator began to ask me a list of questions which I'm sure were routine, given the circumstances. We discussed why I thought I was so full of anger. She wondered if there was something in my life that might be the cause of it. I explained that there was nothing in my present life that made me angry. So we agreed it must be something from my past. At some point in the discussion she claimed that I had not shown up for a previous appointment, which wasn't quite true, and I explained to her why she was wrong to make this accusation. Despite my explanation she didn't apologise for her error and I felt a little aggrieved at that, but our discussion continued.

She took me back to my time in prison and we explored that part of my past for a while. At this point, for some reason I began, rightly or wrongly, to interpret her attitude to me as one of condescension, so I retaliated by addressing her demeaningly as 'pet', to which she immediately objected.

Then she moved on to the subject of Daingean and it was shortly after she started to ask me questions about my experiences there that I lost the head completely. I jumped back, kicked the chair out from under me and simply let out the most hideous roar imaginable. This sickening sound came right from the depths of my stomach. My eyes bulged and I could feel the veins in my neck standing out as if they too were about to explode. I screamed a long-drawn-out 'Fuck you' at her and she became visibly very frightened, her lips trembling in fear. I spotted a snooker table at the far end of the room and in my rage I ran at it and upended it, no mean feat given the weight of such things, roaring at the top of my voice all the time.

Fortunately Jo was outside the room, heard the commotion and came in to see what the disturbance was about. Her arrival promptly shocked me back to my senses. Quickly realising that such violent behaviour was unacceptable and that the police might well be called, I rushed outside, jumped into my Fiat Uno (my first-ever car) and drove off, still raging in torment inside. That incident finally brought home to me how violent I could be and served as a serious warning that I would have to do something to control my outbursts before it was too late.

Ironically, that unsettling incident during my one

and only visit to the Rutland Centre, particularly that raging primal scream, was in itself cathartic and therapeutic. It somehow put me in touch with some aspects of my past and my hidden feelings and it actually started the healing process. I had seen the innocent facilitator as an oppressive authority figure. I felt that here was another one putting me down and I could take no more of it. My response to her was probably the kind of response I would like to have made in the past to people like prison guards, bosses, parents, the brothers in Daingean, cops and so on. But a combination of fear and the repression of my real self meant I had no way of expressing such feelings at all.

My problem was exacerbated by my not realising or accepting that I had such an aversion to many authority figures, even going back to the time I poured paint over the piano in the school. I had turned so much of the hatred back in on myself that it resulted in me having such low self-esteem that I could not think of a single thing I liked about myself when I'd been asked!

Mentally, I was capable of rationalising my anger and accepting that most of my hate figures were simply doing their jobs in difficult circumstances. I would have understood that they in turn had problems that might have driven them into modes of behaviour I often despised. I had to learn that emotions are not rational.

The horrific dreams and nightmares continued, with water a recurring element in many of them. I'd often dreamed I was walking through water. I had one vividly memorable dream about our house in Whitehall in which the small lawn at the front of the house had grass laid out in squares like carpet tiles. I dug under the tiles of grass nearest the house and found the place crawling with maggots. My interpretation of that dream was that it probably related to the fact that the process I was going through was opening the proverbial can of worms, a can that was buried back in my childhood. The water may have been connected to my drinking problem, but the cleansing nature of water might also have been a factor.

I'd been drinking since my mid-teens, and by allowing drink to hide my emotions I'd never given myself the chance to grow. I'd never allowed myself to feel pain. But back then there were not as many avenues of help as there are today. Today people can go on a radio talk show and express their anger and get some reaction and advice that may be very beneficial, but in Ireland not too long ago it was generally regarded as wrong for a man to express his feelings except under the most immediately threatening circumstances.

For me, even today the panics can come at any time without warning. One day walking down O'Connell Street I suddenly felt the onset of panic for no discernible reason. On this occasion I was able to tell myself to stay calm and breathe deeply and it passed. In such attacks I'd feel like I was going to die. My heart would seem as if it was going to stop, the blood would drain from my head, making me feel very faint, and I'd find it hard to breathe. It would be like drowning, and my instinctive reaction would to grab on to something, even a lamp-post would do. But there's no immediate cure other than to face the panic and live with it and hope it passes.

Throughout my difficulties I kept gigging whenever I could get a booking, because music was my main source of income and also because it gave me a sense of continuity. Music was something I could channel my energies into and apply myself to every day. It also provided a partial outlet for the anger inside me. The harmonica in particular was a great way of releasing some of that hatred. Who knows what I would have channelled that anger into had I not had my music?

But having accepted that my alcoholism was not the total cause of all my problems but was instead a reaction to other, more deep-seated problems, I continued to battle to discover what my real problems were. I knew it was going to be a case of peeling back one layer after another and I had no way of knowing how many layers I might have to uncover and whether I would ever get to the core issues at all.

But in due course I learned through various forms of therapy that many of my fears had their roots in the fact that my mother abandoned me in hospital at the age of six. From that point I had cut off contact with my true feelings, so that my anger at her for her affairs, at my father for his drinking and at our deprived situation in general had no outlet. I had bottled it all

173

up and let it fester inside me and wreak havoc for decades and, as if that wasn't enough, my incarceration in Daingean had given me a double load of problems to bear.

Fortunately, whatever the primary reasons for my difficulties, the musicians I played with were all extremely supportive and understanding of my situation. Even though they themselves might be regular drinkers they never put me under any pressure whatsoever and I'll always be grateful for their help and sympathy, especially guys like the keyboardist Gerry Simpson, drummer John Carroll, John Kearns, who played bass guitar, and my long-standing friend and guitarist Gerry Hendricks. They are all fine musicians and decent blokes.

Of course I missed drinking and I've lapsed a couple of time since, but I don't have any yearning for drink now. I don't have a problem sitting in a pub or at a party with other people who might be drinking.

During a period when the band was earning very good money I took a whole month off once to check into the Aiseri rehabilitation centre for alcoholics, just outside Wexford. Neither my agent nor the members of the band were very pleased, and understandably so. This move meant no income for them, or for me, while I was off the road but I was determined to try anything that I thought might heal my life. This showed the extent of my determination to sort things out, especially my relationship with Jo; I was prepared to forego those substantial earnings, to make a personal contribution of £2,000 towards the centre itself and to commit myself to a month in a place with no alcohol, telephones, newspapers, television or any other distraction.

Aiseiri usually takes in people who are just recently off the drink, but I was five years dry at that point, a fact which gave rise to some bemusement among some of the other clients, who assumed that I should not need such treatment. That visit gave me the necessary time to chill out, read, talk, walk in the gardens, enjoy the fresh air and the peace and quiet, explore group therapy and listen to other people, in particularly a lovely woman called Sister Maureen who was in charge of the place and was of tremendous assistance to me. It allowed me to get to know my true self a lot better, and it was an invaluable period of soul-searching and rejuvenation for me, appropriately, given that '*aiséirí*' is Irish for 'resurrection'.

Aiseiri provided me with another significant link in the chain of recovery, as slowly I began to allow myself to feel again. It was if I'd been so deeply hurt I had never allowed myself to really love anyone because I was afraid they'd abandon me and let me down.

Much of this came back to me with a bang only a short while ago when I took my sons Don Elliott and Jackson for a weekend in the country to the Slieve Russell Hotel. Don Elliott, the younger of the two, had gone off to do something else in the hotel while Jackson and I went to play in one of the sports rooms, where we thought he'd have no trouble finding us. But for whatever reason, when the time came Don Elliott couldn't find us, and when he eventually did, I could see the fear in his face, his lips starting to tremble because of his fear that he'd lost his daddy. His fearful face was like a mirror of exactly how lost and abandoned I had felt inside as a child, and how the wounded inner child in me still feels on a permanent basis.

Thankfully, in view of my own childhood suffering, I've learned to become a caring parent to all of my children and I now enjoy a very positive relationship with each one of them. I certainly would never want any of them to go through the agonies I went through. No human being deserves that, even though for a long time I believed I deserved nothing better.

20

THE HEALING PATH

Despite my best efforts, and presumably on account of some of my worst, my marriage to Jo broke up slowly and painfully. We had had two more children after Jordana, who's now in her mid-teens, Jackson, who's eleven, and Don Elliott, now eight. After the split, Jo stayed in the family home and I moved out for good. Over the coming years I would live in a series of flats, most within easy reach of the centre of Dublin, such as on the North Circular Road or George's Street, and I lived in a house in Blanchardstown which is further out on Dublin's west side.

Yet despite all we've been through, together and separately, Jo and I have never not spoken to each other, so there's still a strong bond of friendship and a mutual caring that goes way beyond the fact that she's the mother of three of my children. I still love Jo. She's my best friend, the strongest woman I know and a truly spiritual person.

So although I had initially quit drinking in order to save my marriage, it didn't work out like that in the end. After I'd stopped drinking I came to realise that I'd never made a free, conscious decision at any time in my life. Every time I made a major decision there was some underlying reason for it, so I desperately needed to be detached from all commitments in order to work on myself. I had to do it on my own.

I began to see how I had always put myself down, no matter what I did or how well I really did it, and maybe because I convinced myself that so many others were putting me down too, true or not. I had very little self-worth, virtually no self-esteem and no means of taking a balanced view of my life, my work or myself as a human being.

Acts of kindness from authority figures were such a rare experience for me that I can remember one incident very clearly from when I was in Shanganagh. I was part of a work detail and when I spotted the supervisor had his back turned I slipped off and climbed a chestnut tree for a quiet smoke, a very common occurrence.

But the supervisor spotted my legs sticking down through the branches and he called out, 'Baker, get down out of that tree.' I did as ordered, convinced that I was going to suffer some additional punishment for this. I might be taken up before the governors or given extras duties or a longer sentence or deprived of one of the small privileges which meant so much to us. Anything was possible and I was mentally prepared for the worst as I clambered down.

But when I joined him back on terra firma, instead

of the barrage of harsh words I fully expected he put his arms around me and quietly said, 'Baker, what do you think would have happened if you'd fallen out of that tree?'

Before I could answer he went on, 'I'll tell you what would have happened. You would probably have done some damage to yourself, maybe even broken your leg or your neck. And what do you think would have happened to me? Well, I'd probably lose my job for failing to keep a proper eye on you in the first place. And how would I feed my family then? So can I ask you a question? Would it all have been worth it, inflicting all that pain on all of us, yourself included, just for a quiet smoke?'

I thought about it and reckoned that, all things considered, it wasn't really worth it. But, more importantly, I was also thankful for the quiet and considerate way he had spoken to me, as if he cared about me. I was nineteen years of age yet this was such a rare act of kindness for me to experience from an adult that it made an indelible impression on me. It had a hugely positive impact on me and I'll always be thankful to that decent man. How much different my life might have been if more of my superiors had treated me with similar tenderness and humanity.

But I had to learn to let go of the blame which I directed at the authorities, my so-called betters, my parents and even at myself. I believe that the Holy Spirit guides us towards healing. For example, I think He recently put me into a relationship with Fiona because she goes away all the time! In such situations, the same problem keeps hitting you time and time again until you make the right decision in dealing with it. When you do, you heal that problem and move on to the next step.

The problem gets easier as you develop an awareness of yourself, but it's a slow, painstaking process. I've been hit with very few bolts of inspired lightning along the way. Each gain has been made as a result of dogged effort and application.

Our natural human tendency is to listen to all the therapists and nod our heads in agreement at everything they say as if we understand and accept it all. Intellectually we may accept all they tell us, but without any of it connecting with our emotions, and it's only when it transforms us inside that it can be of lasting healing value. When that true understanding dawns it's like a veil being lifted and we can really see like never before.

In many ways it's like waking up from a dream. In fact, I believe most of us are not just living in a dream state, with no clear awareness of ourselves or our relationship with the world around us, but for many individuals life is a nightmare from which, tragically, we never awaken. Much of my own life was a nightmare, but I was fortunate that a number of factors conspired to set the alarm bells ringing.

Any growth in awareness has to be allowed to take place at its own natural, gradual pace. I know from the extensive reading I've done on the subject and from talking to countless others in the same situation that you can't force it any more than you can force a seed to grow. You can only work on your awareness with diligence and nurture it with care. Nor can you rush headlong to develop an awareness for which you may not even be ready.

In my case I was filled with what's called 'toxic shame', this feeling that I didn't deserve anything better from life and that I didn't really belong to anybody anywhere. We all need a sense of shame, but that's not the same as feeling 'ashamed'. Guilt arises when we feel we made a mistake, but toxic shame convinces you that you are a mistake.

In a book called *A Course of Miracles*, a key part of the reawakening process is called 'choosing again'. That procedure gives you the opportunity to choose another way of dealing with your problem than the way in which you have unsuccessfully attempted to deal with it. It has a deep spiritual dimension to it, but in this healing context you could substitute the word 'spirituality' with the word 'growth'.

There is a theory that our emotions don't grow, that I have the same emotions inside me that I had when I was six. Since I never got the mother's love I craved so badly, as we all do, it became my responsibility to 'parent' myself but the emotions are still the same as they were when I took that role on.

It's been said that all neuroses are a substitute for

legitimate suffering. Part of the process of healing is that acute pain requires you to become aware of yourself, how you act, how you react, how you think, and, most importantly, how you feel. You must make that connection with your deepest feelings, including some which may have lain trapped deep inside you all your life, and it's a very painful process to go through.

I had to learn to accept that other people's opinions of me were really none of my business. Just as I had to let go of the blame I put on other people, I had to let to go of my concern about what other people thought about me. People are entitled to think what they choose about me, as I of them, and it should not concern me how they view me, good, bad or indifferent. But it took a lot of work before I reached that conclusion.

Then too, some friends, quite understandably, will stop me when I'm telling them about my problems and remind me that it's not all bad. They'll tell me I have my health, I'm off the drink, I'm making money, I've got good friends, great kids, a comfortable home, a lot of respect as a musician and as a songwriter and many of the material things I only dreamed of as a kid. But none of that alters the emotional hurt inside. None of it eases the pain, and some find that hard to believe.

21

THE PEOPLE-PLEASER

One of the most obvious manifestations of my co-dependency problem has been what's called 'people-pleasing'. With co-dependency you feel like a lost child, constantly fretting inside. You feel lost and lonely. You feel you need validation but you can't validate yourself. You feel you're not good enough, that you don't deserve anything, that you don't belong. You convince yourself you're a failure. To make matters worse, you're scared in case people find this out about you, and, worse still, you're terrified that it might even be true. So you hide it from yourself as well as everybody else.

Then when you move into a relationship you lose yourself in it and desperately try to become what you think the other person wants you to be. What you should be doing instead is turning back to your inner feelings and pain, and learning to accept them.

I used to do anything if I thought it would please people. I could never say 'no' to anyone if I thought they'd think less of me. My self-esteem depended on others liking me, basically, I suppose, because I didn't like myself. I would do anything to cling on to a relationship in order to avoid feeling abandonment if that relationship ended. Quickly, that fear would turn to obsession with the other person in my attempts to keep the fear at bay. Perversely, that's more likely to scare partners off than keep them with you.

In this way your situation keeps getting more and more convoluted and in the meantime you become more and more co-dependent as your need to get another human being to fix you increases. In its most extreme form it can turn into love addiction and there have been cases of it reaching such extremes as to cause people to murder a loved one.

Fortunately I never reached those depths, but if I thought you didn't like me I'd be in shock and would want to find something, anything, I could do to rectify that situation. I'd give you the shirt off my back, not out of a genuine act of generosity, but so that you'd think, 'I like that Don Baker. He's a really decent bloke, gave me a lovely shirt.' I'd constantly look for approval from outside myself, and that would have been one reason, although perhaps not the principal one, for me becoming an entertainer, as it was the only way I knew through which I might get the crucial applause, approval and attention.

This was a hard lesson, but one I had to learn if I was going to have any spiritual growth. I had to accept that the reason I became a 'people-pleaser' was because I had never found a way of approving of myself. I used to feel like a piece of shit. How can you approve of a piece of shit?

So while it's pleasant when other people say nice things about me, in reality it's more important for me to tell myself I'm a decent bloke or whatever. Somebody else saying it is not what I need, in fact it's irrelevant. So not surprisingly, the thunderous applause, positive reviews and back-slapping never quite worked as the instant fix I thought they should be.

I hope I've come to a reasonably balanced understanding of it all now, but way back then I was blind to my underlying emotions. Sometimes on stage I'd hear the audience's applause and I'd wonder if it might be for the bass player or the drummer or anybody else but me. It's taken me quite a while, with a lot of hard graft, to be able to say, with some honesty and modesty, that maybe I have some real talent as a singer, harp player, guitarist and songwriter. I've felt that slow change creeping up on me over the years, as if I was grudgingly admitting to myself that I might have some value as a human being after all. I must stress that it hasn't come easily.

Nowadays if I do a bad gig, or if the audience reaction is either critical or indifferent, it has a far less negative effect on me than it used to have. Sure, I might be a little disappointed, and that's quite natural, but I've learned not to take it so personally. The fact that the gig might have failed in one sense does not mean that I'm a complete failure as a human being, but I've had to teach myself not to see life on such a critical, personal level. All this might seem like ordinary common sense to most people, but my mindset of yore had little connection with common sense!

My low self-esteem and the behaviour it encouraged sometimes reached ludicrous proportions and often meant that many people saw me as stand-offish and stuck up, too important to talk to them.

In reality the opposite was the case. I remember an occasion when I was out at RTÉ filming a television show which included a group of attractive female models. Instead of chatting to them like a normal human being I studiously avoided them, conscious that they spoke better than me, seemed happier than me, were better educated than me, were probably richer than me, were better dressed than me, appeared more confident than me and were definitely better people than me. But as I was to learn very shortly, I was merely projecting my own feelings onto them in a way that was very misguided and unfair. Instead of acknowledging how I myself felt, I was yet again blaming other people for my feelings, seeing my problems as their problems.

But as it happens, the next I day I went into a fashion store in Dublin where, by coincidence, one of the models whom I'd noticed on the previous day was working. I'd especially observed how well she dressed and assumed that she was very rich to be able to afford such expensive-looking clothes. Although I knew she recognised me from the previous day I continued to ignore her and went around looking at shirts. But talking to her became inevitable, as it was a fairly small store, and when we began to chat I admitted admiring her clothes, remarking that they must have cost her a bundle. I was amazed when she told me that she'd picked every item up very cheaply in different stores and street markets around Dublin – the complete opposite of my narrow-minded assumptions.

I left that store totally bewildered. Here was a very pleasant, honest woman, with absolutely no airs and graces about herself, so I began thinking, 'What exactly is your fucking problem, Baker?' Here I was, giving myself grief based on wildly inaccurate presumptions about other people. I was trying to deal with the imagined opinions and attitudes of people I didn't even know, to an extent that had no connection whatsoever with reality. I was being as unfair to them as I was to myself, and I was guilty of the very faults I was inventing in others while blaming them for the way I felt.

This was another one of those unforeseen occasions that opened the window a little, shed another few rays of light on my own feelings and lead me to reappraise my own self-worth in a realistic way. It was finally beginning to dawn on me that the main problem lay inside my own head, not with others, while I was unfairly projecting my own inner insecurities and prejudices onto those around me.

Of course I'm sure lots of people had told me this

anyway, and I probably nodded my head, and said, 'Oh yeah, sure', and thought I meant it, but it had never really penetrated, maybe because I wasn't quite ready to deal with it with the necessary maturity. We can often intellectualise or verbalise an understanding of some matter when we don't understand it at all deep down, where it's most important.

Let's face it, we're not short of ways of avoiding dealing with things we don't want to deal with. Alcoholism, overwork, smoking, crime, sex and drugs are only the more obvious ways, but we can use the simple means of talking to avoid the real issues as well, pretending we know what's going on when we really don't know and, more importantly, don't want to know. You can't heal what you can't feel, and you can't feel unless you allow yourself to feel.

Of course I've tried many healing methods but not every system works for me, although they might very well help others. For example, I tried acupuncture just once but I don't think it helped me in any way and it didn't connect with my deepest problems. I tried transcendental meditation but something about it didn't gel with me. Nor have I delved too deeply into Eastern religions or meditation practices like Zen, but I haven't closed my mind to them either. As a venerable piece of old wisdom says, 'When the pupil is ready, the teacher appears.'

My problems exist more on an emotional level than on a rational, intellectual one. In my head I can very easily rationalise that if I can play sell-out gigs, write hit songs, act in films, write tutor books and so on, of course I must be reasonably accomplished, but accepting that internally and dealing with that inside myself is where the difficulties have arisen in the past. The Buddhists emphasise 'non-attachment', something I try to practise every day, and I like Kipling's advice to treat the two 'imposters' of triumph and disaster as if they were the same, but I had to learn to stop treating all my triumphs as if they were actually disasters!

Mixed in with my desire to nurture and establish a sense of self-worth is a genuine feeling of humility. I really don't want a fuss made over me and I would hate to be perceived as somebody big-headed or self-important. If a friend, critic or fan told me I did a bad gig last night I would probably have admitted it to myself long before they told me anyway. If they criticised me and I felt it had actually been a good gig I might still become really angry towards them. I'd assume they were just trying to put me down. Sometimes I feel down enough without somebody else trying to put me down further.

I've had to come to terms with a considerable degree of shame at how uncontrollably violent I once was. I abhor violence of any kind, yet I had allowed myself to be goaded into thinking it was the only solution and the 'manly' way to behave. The English poet William Blake wrote:

I was angry with my foe:
I told it not, my wrath did grow.

That about sums me up. I was angry and had nobody to turn to to help me understand the cause of it, so my anger grew to a level that makes me shudder when I think back on it. How I didn't kill somebody was almost a miracle in itself.

I think one of the most significant transformations in my way of thinking came when I released a solo album called *Just Don* in 1998. I finally felt I had developed enough self-confidence to take the risk of exposing my talents without the company and support of a band. It was a breakthrough of some kind, because even five years previously I don't think I would have found the courage to do it, but it was something I had to do for myself. And I did it, and I like it. So there!

22

REBIRTHING AND OTHER THERAPIES

I was in my mid-twenties when my father died, at the age of forty-seven, from lung cancer, presumably not helped by his lifelong smoking habit. My mother died when I was about thirty-one, but I've never been able to grieve her death. I even bought the book *The Courage to Grieve* to help me get on with that process, but it only partially helped. I was able to grieve the loss of my father a little better than that of my mother.

I don't know why there was such a difference in the way I responded to their respective passings, but perhaps I'd switched off my feelings for my mother and put too great a distance between us. I try to deal as honestly as possible with my relationship with my mother later in this book. It may seem unfair, since my father's alcoholism had caused the family far more anguish than anything she ever did, but I have to learn to understand this myself before I can properly heal the hurt I feel that goes back to my relationship with my mother. Maybe because my father was around far less it may have become a case of 'out of sight, out of mind' – and out of heart as well.

Maybe I'll never know, but I'm determined to keep searching for an answer. Part of that relentless search has taken me into many daunting areas, but among the most beneficial I have found are a practice called rebirthing, and therapy on the inner child.

Rebirthing uses a range of techniques that enable the person to relive and face the traumas connected with the various stages of birth, including conception, implantation, life in the womb and delivery. Re-experiencing that process just once can bring us worthwhile insights into why we feel the way we do about core issues in our lives.

When I was about six years free of drink I was advised by a friend to go to Patricia O'Driscoll, who had a fine reputation in this field. Although I had no idea what she really did I was prepared to try anything that might help me.

At our initial therapy session her first request was for me to walk up and down in front of her. A strange request, I thought. After I had done this for a while she said, 'What are you ashamed of?'

I didn't know what she meant, nor what this had to do with the way I walked. So she suggested we swap places and she then imitated the way I had walked. For the first time I realised that I walked with my head down, staring at the ground. I could immediately understand what she'd observed but it had never occurred to me at all. And we started from there, with her advising me that I had to start getting in touch with my inner feelings, no matter how painful that might be.

When Patricia introduced me to the breathing aspect of her work my first problem was an inability to relax and sit still for more than a couple of minutes, a problem I think went back to Daingean and probably beyond. I'd no sooner lie on her couch than I'd be up to make a phone call or something. I'd keep checking my watch and asking her was she nearly finished, all in my anxiety to avoid facing and feeling the reality of what was buried deep inside. When the session was over I'd rush out and drive off in a hurry, yet I kept coming back! It took me a full eighteen months before the therapy began to take effect and I finally let go and broke through the barrier.

It is believed that many of our behaviour patterns, and maybe many illnesses too, are triggered by early traumas we have experienced. Part of the rebirthing technique involves deep breathing and this has taught me that instead of looking outside for somebody or some 'thing' to fix me, I breathe into it and allow the child in me to deal with it.

For the first time I noticed how the words 'birth' and 'breath' are quite close in sound. The writer Anthony de Mello describes the breath as our best friend. Sometimes the breathing brings on a feeling of deep sadness. I'm lucky in that I can cry very easily. But one thing I can't do, which I'd dearly love to do, is to really let myself fall apart and shake and sob on the floor for about an hour. I'm convinced I'd come out of that a transformed man, but the 'John Wayne' philosophy so dominant in Irish culture during my formative years still manages to block that. That notion that real men should not allow themselves to feel is such nonsense when you consider that in truth it takes real courage to feel and to risk the fear and everything else that goes with a true emotional experience of the world. I know that now, but it's one thing knowing it, another matter to live it.

I spent two years with an Englishwoman called Jay Silvers participating in various psychotherapeutic techniques, including regression therapy, holotropic therapy (more popularly known as primal therapy), transactional analysis (healing the inner child) and transpersonal therapy (cutting the ties that bind). I attended Jay once a week during the two years. When I began the therapy with her she warned me that there would come a time when there would be a third person in the room with us; that I'd think it was her although it would be somebody else from my past. As the therapy progressed this prophecy slipped from my mind. Part of Jay's technique required me to do some fast breathing similar to the sharp intakes of breath we take when we get a fright. This was intended to stir up feelings and memories. One momentous night during a session of such breathing I suddenly stopped.

Jay asked, 'Why have you stopped, Don?'

'You're too rough,' I said.

'Who's too rough?'

'I told you, you're too rough, you're just browbeating me. I don't want to do this any more.'

But she kept asking me, 'Who's too rough, Don?' and I kept saying, 'I told you. You are.' Until one further time she repeated the question and I replied, 'The nurse is too rough.'

She said, 'Where are you now, Don?'

'I'm in hospital.'

'What's happening?'

'They're stitching my head,' I said, and with that I began to shake.

Jay took my hand and reassured me, 'It's OK. Tell me what's going on.'

'The nurse is holding my head still, but I want to look at the stuffed parrot on the perch behind me. I keep twisting my head back.' Then I went quiet.

'What's happened? Tell me.'

'My father split my head open with a steel sugar bowl and they're stitching my head but I don't remember getting here. I can feel the hostility of the doctors. I feel that it's all my fault.'

She then leaned forward and whispered in my ear, 'You know those anxiety attacks when you imagine you have a brain tumour or that you're about to have a brain haemorrhage? Well, Don, you'll never have another attack like that again.'

Oddly, I still can't remember visiting the hospital to have my head attended to all those years back after I had intercepted that sugar bowl my father intended for my mother's head. But my sister remembers me being taken somewhere. She's obviously right because I actually had to have twenty-seven stitches for the wound. Whether I was detained overnight is something she can't verify, but I have no recollection whatsoever of having my head-wound atttended to. Somehow I had erased that memory completely from my mind, but the therapy had reawoken part of it. That sugar bowl blow may have been the root cause of the concerns I experienced during my anxiety attacks, and as Jay promised, I never had them again to the same extent as before.

Jay's techniques were of enormous benefit to me. Finally one evening I walked into her office for another session and she greeted me with an outstretched hand and just said, 'Don, you're finished here. I'm so proud to know you and you're one of the most courageous people I've ever met. I want you to know that, but I can do no more for you.'

John Wayne wasn't in it as I swaggered out of her house that night!

23

IN THE NAME OF THE FATHER . . .

As I explained earlier, I found acting to be a far more therapeutic exercise for me than music. The fact that it enables me to pour my emotional self into a role without the same practical restrictions that music presents is truly liberating for someone like me, who has found it so hard all his life to express his deepest feelings. So my appearance in *In the Name of the Father* was a real boost, not just in relation to the acting itself, but because I had the good fortune to work with such true professionals in such a highly acclaimed film.

My involvement in that film came about almost by accident. The well-known Dublin director Jim Sheridan and the actor Daniel Day-Lewis used regularly to come to hear me doing gigs at a venue called The Speakeasy in what is now the fashionable part of Dublin, Temple Bar. Three hundred people would squeeze in every week until they would have to close the doors. You'd see the sweat running down the walls!

Daniel is a big blues fan and an extremely down-to-earth bloke, so we hit it off immediately. Jim's a true

Dubliner like myself, so we each knew where the others were coming from all the time. We'd frequently pop next door to Fat Freddy's pizza place for a bite, a chat and a laugh. My ex-wife Jo would laugh at Daniel when he'd say he wished he had my talent, given his own prodigious talents.

At about the same time, my cousin Pamela Scully, who's a big Samuel Beckett fan and was then running a theatre company in Dublin, invited me to take on the role of the blind character Hamm in a staging of Beckett's *Endgame* she was producing at the Andrew's Lane Theatre. I agreed on condition I could wear dark glasses, as I was not confident I could successfully carry off the pretence of being blind if the audience could see my eyes.

After a dinner for my birthday, at which the guests included both Jim and Daniel, I invited them to join me at a gig by the man I rate as the greatest harmonica player in the world, the West Virginia country star Charlie McCoy, who was playing in Dublin at the Break for the Border venue. As I had anticipated, I was totally blown away by McCoy's performance at that gig, but Daniel and Jim would have none of it and kept telling me I was far better than McCoy, although I tried to explain the differences in our respective styles. We got into a bout of harmless slagging of the 'What do you know about music? More than you know about acting.' variety, during which I told them that I was rehearsing for the Beckett play. They were obviously quite surprised, never having thought of me as an actor. (Neither had I till then!) Nor did I suspect that they would have other plans for me.

About a week later I got a phone call asking me to meet Daniel and Jim immediately in the Royal Hospital in Kilmainham to discuss a possible part for me in a film for which where they were holding auditions. I had heard nothing about the film other than that it featured a prison, so I went along, presuming they had a part requiring somebody to play a harmonica in jail. I foresaw myself having my head shaved, being dressed in regulation prison uniform and perhaps wailing a few lonesome tunes on the harmonica. This prospect quite excited me and I was eagerly looking forward to it. But when I got to the set Jim straight away presented me with a script and told me to take a walk around the garden and read the part of Joe McAndrew.

Never having read a script before I was quite surprised and nervous about this proposal. When I eventually came back onto the set he asked me to read the script with Daniel playing opposite me, but being a total novice at this I found it quite hard to follow the script and act the part at the same time. Seeing how much I was struggling with this new discipline, Jim took the script away and suggested I improvise.

Immediately I laid into Daniel with the cameras running. We improvised about six minutes of dialogue and when we finished, everybody on the set seemed positively shocked with my performance, so I jokingly asked, to much laughter, 'Right, so do I get to play the harmonica or what?'

Some days later I heard through the grapevine that I was going to play the role of Joe McAndrew in *In the Name of the Father*, the film about the Guildford Four and their unjust treatment at the hands of the British authorities. Some time afterwards I received a call at home from Jim himself to confirm he was indeed giving me a part, but not the one I'd auditioned for because Gabriel Byrne wanted it. I had no qualms about playing second fiddle to such a talented actor as Gabriel, and I was quite happy to accept a more minor role, with or without playing the harmonica.

The part I was now told I was going to play was that of an Englishman, so I began to fret about my ability to put on a convincing English accent, and I agreed with Jim, after some discussion, that a Cockney accent would be the easiest for me. So off I went to the voice tutor Peter Gunn, who advised me to study the accents of Michael Caine and Bob Hoskins. I then brought a woman over from London who came to all my gigs. Whenever I'd meet her I'd try to write down phonetic script for the way Cockneys spoke. I was really taking this acting lark very seriously, all for the mere possibility of saying one or two lines! I'm told I even started to introduce my songs in a very odd English accent!

I'd drop down to the set nearly every day, realising for the first time that what a slow business film-making is. Each day I expected to be called on to do my bit, but that did not happen yet.

Then the phone at home rang once again. Jo answered, to find it was Jim, so, assuming for some reason that I was going to be dropped, I signalled for her to say I wasn't in. I had suddenly decided that I wasn't an actor after all and it wasn't going to work. Luckily, Jim twigged I was there and got me on the phone to offer me the part as originally planned, because, for some reason, Gabriel was not going to do it after all.

Jim wanted me immediately on the set in Merrion Square. When I got there I started apologising to Jim for not having brought any clothes and saying that I hadn't had time to wash my hair and so on. He laughed and roared at me, 'Don, this is a film set we have here. We've got a whole fucking wardrobe of clothes and make-up and everything you need! We've done this before, you know!'

And that's how I ended up with a fairly prominent role in *In the Name of the Father*. I was fascinated by the tricks they used on set to give me a very convincing three-day growth of beard and to alter some very ill-fitting clothes to suit my build. When I eventually started to shoot scenes I got stuck into it with gusto, and I got so animated during one scene that I lost my watch. I was thrilled when Daniel threw his arms around me and said, 'Don, I know you're going to bring something very personal and very special to this film.'

Given my own family background I could readily identify with the film's anger at the tragic, real-life injustice it dealt with. The authorities can fuck us all up and there's so little the weak and powerless can do to redress that injustice.

Obviously, the jail scenes I featured in brought me back to my own time in prison. In fact it was during one of them that I discovered that this acting lark could be rather dangerous. It was the scene in which two English prisoners threaten me over breakfast, and when I hit one of them it sparks a minor riot.

While we were rehearsing this scene I spotted the stunt coach teaching one of the actors how to wield a snooker cue, getting him really psyched up for the scene. This brought me back to my street-fighting days and since I was to be in that same scene I became quite nervous about it. My fears proved justified, because when the guy with the snooker cue went to hit the wall above my head as he was meant to do, part of it caught me on the side of the head. Down I went, genuinely out cold on the ground, with my head bleeding. The nurse on standby on the set was rushed into action and brought me to with smelling salts or something. My first thoughts on waking up were that I'd been so badly injured that I'd lose the part, but it turned out to be less serious an injury than it had seemed at first.

All in all I found playing the role a very emotional experience, and when they had finished filming my role I collapsed into the arms of Daniel Day-Lewis and sobbed. Daniel thought it was because, in his own method-acting approach to his part, he appeared to really turn against me, but the real reason I broke down was because the scenes had helped me partly to reconnect with what I had repressed for so long. Having to act tough in the film reminded me of what I was doing in real life to avoid my deeper emotions. I had dropped my defences for maybe only as much as ten minutes, but the effect was startling and there was a great deal of healing in what happened.

Shortly afterwards Daniel made me a present of a book called *The Drama of the Gifted Child*, which tells the story of a female therapist who got in touch with her inner feelings only when she took up painting. I suppose I've tried to use my songwriting to achieve a similar effect.

Appearing in *In the Name of the Father* brought me other unexpected blessings. It was while she was watching the film that Fiona, who's originally from Tuam, was, she subsequently told me, first attracted to me. After we had nearly met twice, our paths finally crossed in 1995 in the Traveller's Friend in Castlebar in County Mayo. This took place during the 'Four for the Road' tour of Ireland in which I played with such stalwart Irish performers as Finbar Furey, Mick Hanly and Jimmy McCarthy.

Fiona and I started living together in early 1996 and we became engaged on 30 December 1997. We've had our ups and downs, just as people do in all relationships, but I'm really grateful to her because she's been a major factor in helping me see my own problems much more clearly and face up to my inner demons.

The fact that Fiona has a degree in psychology has given her a generous empathy with my own situation, and she has consistently helped me work through my difficulties with tremendous love, understanding and dedication For this I will be grateful to her as long as I live. Obviously I also owe thanks to Jim Sheridan, who indirectly brought us together by giving me, a totally untried actor, that role in his film. I probably never thanked him for this.

After the good notices I received for my performance in *In the Name of the Father* I landed a major part in a thirteen-part television series called *Mia* which has already been shown six times on Spanish television. Whereas in *In the Name of the Father* I played a cold, fairly emotionless character, my part in *Mia* was the opposite, running the whole gamut of emotions from laughter to tears, remorse, anger and sadness. I played opposite the legendary Claudia Cardinale, who had the role of the mother of the illegitimate child of the title. I was her lover in our late teens before I left to go off to war. The series was set in a small Irish fishing village and I had many scenes in which I could show my emotions. Some vividly brought my mother back to life again and it was a thoroughly positive and therapeutic experience. Seeing some of my scenes played back to me came as a real shock, as I'd never suspected I could express such naked emotion. Although the series was set in Ireland it hasn't been shown here yet.

I also had a part in *Soft Sands, Soft Seas* and in *Sunset Heights*, the latter a thriller set in Northern Ireland for which I was cast as the Mayor of Derry. More recently I filmed a part in *Mercy* in Lisbon, Portugal, and I took the part of a crook in *Underworld*. I have to admit I've enjoyed every second of my film career and am thankful not just for the experience, the exposure and the money, but also for the much-needed emotional release it has brought me.

Only very occasionally, and then usually in my harmonica-playing, have I ever come close to reaching the hidden depths inside me. I was singing a John Prine song called 'Sam Stone' one time and when I came to the line 'There's a hole in daddy's arm where all the money goes' it really got to me like nothing else when I related it to my own father. But those rare musical experiences do not excavate my soul the way acting does.

The Rolling Stones drummer Charlie Watts was once asked to reflect on the twenty-five years the band had been in existence. 'Five years playing, and twenty years waiting around,' was his laconic reply.

And that about sums up life in the entertainment business in general, not just music. I've referred earlier to the tedium of recording, but I don't think it compares to the time you spend hanging about waiting for takes on a film set.

On several occasions I've been invited to contribute

some harmonica to a film soundtrack, a television commercial, radio commercial or somebody else's record, like one of Christy Moore's, for example. Quite often I'll come into the studio, they'll play the track to me and then I'll improvise a piece which I think is appropriate for the piece and which I hope they'll like. Quite often I'll get it in a couple of takes. In fact there have been times when I've hit it on the button first time round, but either way it's all usually done so fast that I don't even get a chance to sit down.

Oh how I wish acting in films could be like that, although common sense tells me that it could never be. Instead you spend endless hours waiting around to be called on to the set and then you may have to repeat a scene countless times until the director is happy with a take. I usually pass the time reading a book, and some actors use the spare time to learn a language or for some other serious studying. You also learn that you have to be patient with your fellow actors as you hope they'll be patient with you and your missed cues, forgotten lines and other screw-ups.

Acting is not merely a matter of speaking the lines in the right order. I don't really class myself as an actor at all since I've never gone to acting classes and I've no experience of stage acting either, so I prefer to see myself as a performer. So I was intrigued to learn from different directors how the merest gesture, the raising of an eyebrow or the curl a lip, can add weight and meaning to a line.

In doing a particular scene you have to remember all those details – turn your mouth into a slight leer when you say that word or turn your face slightly away from the camera between those two phrases, and so on. It can become very confusing when you're new to it and it can also be very stressful, but once the camera starts rolling it creates such an adrenaline rush that you're quite disappointed when the scene finishes.

You learn to live permanently with the possibility that the great two-minute scene you spent three days getting right might eventually end up on the cutting-room floor, not because there was anything intrinsically wrong with it, but merely because it did not fit into the director's overall shape for the film when it came to the editing stage.

I had a different type of disappointment when I was cast for the part of Sir John Gage in the film *Elizabeth*, about the 16th-century British queen. I was flown across to England for auditions, which in itself was a trying experience since I knew I was up against some experienced English actors. So I was delighted when my agent called to tell me I'd been chosen for the part.

When filming proper was about to start, some months later, I flew back to England again and spent quite some time thinking myself into the part and then getting kitted out in the costume of the time, including those pumpkin-like trousers you see so often in movies set during Tudor times. But soon after I arrived on the set the director took a couple of quick looks at me and decided there and then that I had been wrongly cast and that was that. Still, there was the consolation of the substantial fee which had been negotiated by my agent, but I would have enjoyed the challenge of that role.

Perhaps because the story was set on the northside of Dublin, where I had grown up, I was more disappointed not to be cast in *The Commitments*. I was in the running for the part of Joey the Lips but didn't get it. Later the film's director, Alan Parker, after having seen me in *In the Name of the Father*, kindly dropped me a line congratulating me, as did Ross Hubbard, the casting agent, who had opted not to use me for *The Commitments*. You have to expect that, as in music and most areas of life, you win some and you lose some, and whether you win or lose you have to accept the outcome with good grace.

We filmed a lot of the television series *Mia* down in Baltimore in County Cork. I was familiar with Claudia Cardinale, especially from her appearance in *How the West Was Won*, Sergio Leone's blockbuster western made in the late sixties, and lots of other films I'd seen her in, so it was a tremendous honour filming with her.

But some of my dearest memories about the actual filming centre around the Italian director, who was a very emotional man, to say the least. Irish people are not very demonstrative by nature, so I'm not sure what the fine people of Baltimore made of his histrionics.

If I do a scene well I certainly appreciate a pat on

the back, like everybody else, but that was never enough for my Italian friend. Immediately after I had finished filming one particular scene down at the waterfront by the pier I heard him roaring, 'Get me down! Get me down!' as he insisted on being lowered from his usual perch overlooking the set in his director's crane. When that was done and he had arrived safely back on the ground he came charging along the beach towards me shouting, 'Belleeseemo, belleeseemo, beautiful, beautiful,' at the top of his voice, with tears streaming down his face. He lifted me clean off my feet and planted kisses all over my face. I know it's a cliché but I genuinely didn't know where to look on that occasion.

After another scene we had shot in a bar he came over to me, once again with his tear-stained face, and said, 'You-a make-a me cry, you-a make-a me cry!' over and over. I suppose I should be glad he was pleased with my performance, but I'm not given to that kind of outward show of emotion. Even when I go on talk shows on television I dread the prospect that the host is going to plant a few wet kisses all over my face. This seems to be a very recent development in Ireland, an affectation we've imported from somewhere else. The French and Russians do it all the time, but a firm handshake will do me, thanks all the same.

But if you're part of a film crew for months and months on end, working under stress every day, the people bond like a well-knit family. You realise how dependent you are on each other, and when the camera starts to roll everybody wants to do their bit perfectly so as not to let the rest of the team down. So I can sympathise when I see somebody getting a bad review because, irrespective of the quality of the end product, I know how much blood, sweat and tears has gone into the making of it.

Incidentally, while a writer in the English newspaper *Independent on Sunday* claimed I should have got an Oscar for my part in *In the Name of the Father* and the respected film critic Barry Norman in England and others in the British media singled me out for much praise, I rated hardly a mention in the Irish media. Yet I meet a lot of people in Ireland who know more about me from that film than from my music career. That has always struck me as strange, especially since the film was an anti-British-establishment movie, but perhaps I shouldn't read too much into it.

Seeing myself up on the big screen in that film was an amazing experience and I deliberately went to see it again in a Dublin cinema. In a sense I was attempting the impossible, trying to see how my performance as Joe McAnthony actually looked to a paying filmgoer out for a night's entertainment. Like a proper movie fan I bought myself a big box of popcorn and some ice cream and sat excitedly at the back of the cinema. I was very keen to observe the audience's reaction as well. Overall they seemed to thoroughly enjoy the film, but I was actually quite astonished at the response to the scene involving me and the billiard cue, when a few lads in front of me jumped up and vehemently roared, 'Come on, get that fucker, Joe!'.

In some ways it was scary to witness such an emotional and aggressive reaction, while in other ways it was a compliment in that they were so convinced by my portrayal of the character. But it reminded me of the times when I used to go to the films as a kid. We used to refer to the hero as 'the chap' and if there was someone sneaking up behind him we'd stand up and roar out to warn him, as if we believed he could actually hear us. So film somehow has the ability to enable us to suspend reality. We know the characters on the screen are played by actors, and we know they can't hear us anyway, yet it doesn't stop us somehow thinking we can communicate with them.

Maybe that's the magic of cinema.

My laterst foray into films, playing the role of a gangster in *Underworld*, was given a boost when the film went on national release in the cinemas in Ireland towards the end of 1999. The story is set in Dublin's gangland and it's yet another example of an aspect of my early life having an echo later on in my professional career.

24

. . . And of the Mother

After years of therapy of various kinds I finally had to admit that most of my emotional problems could be traced back to my relationship with my mother and the secret thoughts I had about her. I had to go through much pain and torment to make real contact with my true inner self, and what I learned when I made that connection startled me and shocked me very profoundly at first.

This may be more common than we, especially men, want to admit, but the ramifications of the mother-son relationship can have an extraordinary, lifelong impact – and not always for the good. This subject has absorbed great minds for centuries, and most people are familiar with the concept of the Oedipus complex, which theorises that all sons want to have sexual intercourse with their mothers. One of the biographers of the English poet Lord Byron has speculated that the poet's conviction of the unreliability of all women might be traced back to his mother's tempestuous changes of mood. So who knows for sure what traumas can be visited upon us in the early years of that crucial relationship?

As I've said earlier, my mother was a glamorous, flirtatious woman. I'm sure she was quite promiscuous and might even have been addicted to men and to sex in the same way I later became addicted to alcohol. When I look back it seems there were men around her nearly all the time, although the full import of that only hit me later.

I think I was intimidated by her. I can't look back at our relationship and think of it as a normal mother-son relationship. This was not just because, given the circumstances of my father's alcoholism, I had taken on the role of father to the family, but perhaps also because I may have unconsciously lusted after her.

This never manifested itself in any kind of physicality, and I don't think I knew what my true feelings towards her were at the time, but I know now that I felt bad then about the way I felt about her. Maybe even as children we can sense that a person is highly sexually charged, even if we can't express the idea that way.

I felt from childhood that my feelings were suspect enough that they should be kept to myself but, as I explored my inner feelings more deeply, memories of events which I had long buried began to resurface. I recall, for instance, a time when I had committed some misdemeanour that had come to the attention of the police. This was followed by the usual series of visits to our house by the local cops. But these visits, especially by one particular garda, continued on the pretext that he was keeping an eye to me to make sure I was getting up to no more mischief.

On the surface, this was a noble gesture, but then I would see him and my mother talking and laughing at the hall door. Their joviality didn't square with his supposed interest in my welfare. They would disappear surreptitiously inside the house and all would be quiet for a while. I was probably too young to know what they were up to, but inside I knew something was wrong, and I didn't like the way it made me feel.

I never felt more alone than when one of my mother's lovers would call to the house and I'd be sent upstairs and everything would go totally quiet downstairs. On one occasion I was enraged enough to open an upstairs window and shout after one individual as he left, 'Don't come back here. We don't want you.' My mother dragged me in from the window and simply told me to go to sleep, although I doubt very much whether I was able to sleep, with the intense feelings of loneliness I was suffering.

My sister Catherine recently recalled that as a child she was in the local park with my mother one day when a man arrived who was obviously a close friend of my mother. After a brief chat he gave Catherine money to buy sweets in the local shop, but when she returned earlier than they had anticipated she found them having sex in the long grass.

This and other incidents confirm that my own suspicions were not based on some boyish fantasy. Unfortunately, not only did these suspicions make me feel bad inside, but I had nobody to talk to about them even if I had been able to verbalise them. So all these complex feeling were heaped on top of the fears of abandonment that had begun to trouble me from that first hospital visit when I was six. Perhaps my concern about my mother's sexual activities added to this fear, since each of those relationships brought with it the possibility that she would leave me for another man. Of course I had already been abandoned emotionally, but the fear of permanent physical abandonment was an even greater terror.

Somehow I could sense that she was not a normal mother. She was always extravagantly made up. She would regularly tell me some of the things certain men had said about her – that she had fine legs, a fantastic figure or whatever. I don't think any child, boy or girl, expects his mother to talk to him or her like that. There seemed to be no boundaries between her and me in relation to sexual matters. Whereas most women, and indeed most men, adopt a modesty and a sense of privacy around their dressing and undressing, she would quite openly allow me to see her almost totally naked, putting on her nylon stockings, bra or knickers. Whether she was simply showing off or teasing me or whether she just didn't care who saw her in what stage of undress, I'll never know. I do know that such behaviour had an impact on me and certainly aroused in me some kind of sexual feelings towards her. But I was too young to be conscious either of her sexuality or of my own, so for me as a child it was all very confusing and damaging.

How often back then I wished that she would be normal and love me as a child should be loved. In a more mundane way, I would have given anything to see her wearing an apron, just like all the other mums I saw in the neighbourhood.

To add to my woes, her attractiveness was obvious even to the kids in my class at school. They would regularly ask me with a snigger if she was coming to collect me so that they could ogle her. They too could sense her sexuality. Few men could be in her company without flirting with her or passing some remark of a sexual nature, often accompanied by lewd guffaws or suggestive sniggering.

I think I felt threatened by her sexuality, and even if she had no intention of hurting me, I was the one left bearing the scars of her behaviour when all I desired was to feel loved and wanted. There were moments when I thought that such love was going to be forthcoming, only to have my expectations cruelly dashed.

There was one event that happened after I'd run away for the umpteenth time and was making a tentative move back towards the house, craving for her not only to want me back but also to show me some love and understanding this time. She met me on the road outside the house and seemed all-forgiving, telling me not to be afraid, to come and have my dinner and everything would be all right.

I was reluctant to trust her, as I edged my way along the hedge, but she somehow convinced me that this time she meant it. So I went in and sat down to a typical dinner of sausages and mashed potatoes with the other kids and everything seemed fine. I felt that maybe at last she had some compassion for me.

But not for long. As soon as I had finished eating, her attitude was totally transformed. She dragged me up the stairs by the hair, shouting and screaming obscenities at me, took off my clothes and beat the shit out of me with a belt.

When she was finished she locked me in the room as further punishment and took my clothes away to stop me from going off again. Of course the physical beating hurt me but this was nothing compared to the ache of betrayal, and I was overcome by the need to be off again. I searched the room for clothes to wear and found a pair of my sister's slacks and a pair of her runners. Although they were several sizes too small for me I squeezed into them and escaped through the window, a ten-year-old child off again into the great big world in search of love, since the proper source of that love, my mother, was emotionally unavailable to me. Maybe I became addicted even at that early age addicted to getting into trouble as the only answer to questions I didn't understand.

My mother left me feeling remorseful and guilty over the feelings I had for her, yet I had no way of acknowledging this and went into total denial instead. Even when through therapy as an adult I began to touch on these dormant feelings I tried to minimise them rather than face them fully. In this culture we're taught to honour our parents, so that pressure further prevented me from allowing myself to make contact with my true feelings. Instead, I would try to convince myself that it was me who was bad.

When my father, in his rages, called her a prostitute, I wasn't sure what he meant, although I knew it was a bad thing. In the fifties in Dublin there was a notorious brothel called Dolly Fossetts and the name would be the subject of crude remarks or dirty jokes. But I used to be terrified that, when my father called my mother a prostitute or a whore, maybe it was true and she was working somewhere like Dolly Fossetts.

So while it may seem irrational to others, as well as to myself, I've harboured a deep-seated mistrust of women all my life that has tainted even my most loving friendships with extraordinary depths of insecurity. Until I learned where all this stuff was coming from there were times in relationships when I tried to justify my mistrust by blaming my partner and exaggerating the effects of some trivial slight. I would blame her for how I felt and justify my behaviour in that way rather than having to accept the truth. I became angry, possessive, controlling and jealous to such an irrational degree that

it must have mystified anybody w.
close relationship.

I had yet to discover the truth of it, and I was alw.,
trying to fix 'the hole in my soul' by means that were
outside myself. To me, in my appalling ignorance, it
seemed quite simple. If a woman would only do exactly
what I wanted her to do then I'd be okay. Today I can
see this as age-regression, going back to old feelings
from the past, but it set me up for co-dependency and
I buried my feelings in alcoholism. Accepting where all
my problems were coming from was the first, albeit
painful, step towards understanding myself and allowing
myself to grow. Until I hit on those inner feelings I had
no true awareness of myself and wrote a song called
'Running from Freedom' about my earlier refusal to deal
with my feelings.

Because of my feelings about my mother I've never
had a successful relationship with any woman. On a
mental level it all seems perfectly natural that I should
have responded in the way I did, but that realisation
itself does not heal the pain or give me back that lost
childhood. Nor does it ease the inability to manage the
buried feelings which often surface without warning,
even today, and cause havoc in my head and in my
dealings with others. Sometimes today when I speak
about these matters I can feel all the grief lodging on
my chest, and it affects my respiration quite badly. For
my own sanity and for the sake of my own growth I
have to face these facts. Rejecting my own feelings

...art of myself. No matter ...ght try to dress it up, my ...was and there's nothing to be ...y longer the extent to which I ...behaviour. Nor is there any advan- ...y feelings towards her, irrespective of ...eelings are socially acceptable or not.

U... ...ding where all my problems stem from at least give... me an explanation for them, but it still doesn't stop me driving women away from me because they are essentially dealing with an adult spurred by the feelings of a child. I become afraid of other men in case they take my woman away from me. It's my main ambition to heal this, because I don't like being a co-dependent, depending emotionally on another human being to the extent that I do whenever I get involved in a relationship.

But I can take some comfort in knowing that I'm finally beginning to take responsibility for my feelings, and I feel no shame in making these admissions. Nor do I want to get stuck in the rut of blaming my mother for it all, but it is important to place the responsibility where it lies.

25

I Wish I Had Religion

For my 1989 album *Almost Illegal* I recorded one of my own songs, 'I Wish I Had Religion'. All of my own songs are autobiographical and written from an emotional standpoint rather than an intellectual one. Although you might get the opposite impression from its title, 'I Wish I Had Religion' was not a cry from the heart for some kind of organised group to attach myself to, nor was I seeking some set of precepts with which to brainwash myself.

To me now, religion means spirituality, and spirituality in turn means growth. Let's face it, most people in Ireland, although they might profess to follow a particular faith, really only attach themselves to the religion of their parents in the same casual way they might inherit a family heirloom. If you asked them about their religion, most of them would be unable to tell you much of substance about it.

I can't say what the Irish education system is like today in this regard, but in my time we were taught much about religion but nothing about spirituality, and the two are vastly different in my book. Religion was taught almost as a discipline which we had to learn and then follow like automatons under threat of eternal damnation. Sexuality was never discussed at all, neither in school nor in the home. In fact I don't believe that either of my parents would have been capable of talking to any of us about sex in a healthy way. They would have been far too embarrassed.

Like most people in this state, I was born a Catholic, but there's no way I could describe myself as one today. I see myself simply as an individual with a range of views and beliefs who will keep growing and changing until the day I die, because I don't feel that the search for truth ends. To adopt any one religion would suggest to me that I had stopped growing, and that would be pointless – and the opposite of spirituality as I understand it.

I've seen the enormous power of religion misused by the unscrupulous in order to wield authority over others for their own gain. Instead of being taught exclusively about one religion from the earliest possible age I would prefer a situation where we were allowed to test the rightness and wrongness of what different religions and philosophies have to offer.

Most of the accusations that are habitually levelled at what are often described as 'cults' could also at times be applied to the major religions, and I have never really understood the basic difference between religions and cults. They all try to shape us from the earliest possible age. But what's the point in teaching kids who are too young to understand right from wrong, as I was, to admit committing sins 'through my fault, through my fault, through my most grievous fault', while beating their chests in self-chastisement? To subject innocent kids to this is a questionable practice and I can't see what it has to do with true spirituality.

I've seen religion used to divide people from one another, and we can see the consequences of such divisions on our own doorstep in the conflict in Northern Ireland and in the recurring trouble spots around the globe, such as the Balkans, the Middle East, India, Pakistan and the Far East. Millions have murdered, millions have been murdered, in the name of one faith or another. M. Scott Peck, who wrote *The Road Less Travelled*, claims that one's mental state and one's spiritual state are two sides of the same coin. Each can nurture the other. Work on one and the other benefits. But our culture tells us, and especially tells men, to avoid dwelling too much on what goes on in our minds and in our hearts.

Our society provides numerous opportunities for physical exercise, from field sports to aerobics, cycling and mountain-climbing. But are there any classes or activities that cater for our mental health? Not as far as I can tell. I remember an RTÉ TV programme in which the Labour politician Michael D. Higgins chatted with the late Noel Browne, who was Minister for Health in the 1950s. They discussed the view that Ireland had been colonised twice, once physically, politically and economically by the British, and then mentally, spiritually and emotionally by the Catholic Church. I think that neatly encapsulates the problems I and others have had to face. The guilt and shame I felt growing up, merely because I was from a poor family and had an alcoholic father, resulted from an intolerance and lack of charity ingrained in our society, and which was not tempered by any religious sensibility.

A long time back I decided I wanted no part in organised religion. I've looked instead for something more substantial than a blind faith, and that unremitting search has played a major role in my recovery from alcoholism. It has also helped me deal with my other problems. A genuine religious conviction has its value, but at best I think it can only help us take a couple of steps in the right direction on what is a journey thousands of miles long. I firmly believe that ultimately we have to walk those thousands of miles on our own.

Much Christian teaching revolves around forgiveness, but it's usually forgiveness of other people, whereas I've come to believe that forgiving ourselves within can be far more important. If we forgive ourselves for our own shortcomings we put aside all the anger and guilt with which we daily crucify ourselves.

Just as I've been addicted to alcohol, some people seem to crave a safe, cosy explanation of the big issues in life. But believing in something of itself doesn't make it true, no matter how hard you believe it. I've seen how the very word 'God' and all the baggage that comes with it can for some people be a block to spirituality.

Perhaps all religions offer some part of a great truth. But for me, peace of mind is the most important thing, perhaps the only real treasure any of us can hope to find in this life. The fact that I've found some internal peace, if only some and only lately, is a great comfort to me and an encouragement to continue the search.

As I wrote in the song 'I Wish I had Religion', I feel there has to be a reason for living and dying. I can't comprehend a world where it makes no difference whether you are the most vicious genocidal dictator or a good-living, compassionate individual.

My attitude to politics is quite similar to my feelings about religion. I have no time for the political tactics that divide societies everywhere. Politicians often seem more intent on point-scoring than on improving the quality of life in the societies they are supposed to serve.

It can hardly be a coincidence that in Ireland we've observed in recent years an increasing scepticism about both the established churches and our political system.

26

THE WINNER IN YOU

The title of this book was inspired by one of my favourite songs, 'Winner In You', which I've played countless times in concert and which I released on my 1993 album *No Nonsense*. I was introduced to the song by Johnny Norris when we were touring Germany. But I didn't perform it in Ireland until one night when my guitarist, Gerry Hendricks, broke a string and instead of keeping the audience waiting I started to sing it without Gerry, accompanying myself on my own guitar. It brought an amazing reaction and I was persuaded to record it straight away. Apart from Johnny's, I've never heard another version of it, but I know it was written by two people called Holyfield and Williams.

The song opens with the lines:

I ought to know what it's like to lose a love.
I've done it enough and I ought to know.
Then you came my way
and tore away the fear and pain.
I won't lose again.

This time I know
I've got a winner in you.

In contemplating its lyrics and relating them to my own life I began to wonder why, as the song relates, it's so important for the narrator to feel he has to find a winner in somebody else. Why not find a winner in yourself, I thought, and that set me off down a whole new road of thought, which led to me realising that it's not right to be dependent on another human being for your emotional security. Making important changes to yourself is, to borrow criminal parlance, 'an inside job'. Nobody else can make those changes for you. The journey from the head to the heart is the longest journey most of us will ever undertake, and I can certainly vouch for the truth in that.

When I'd reached the rock-bottom all alcoholics have to reach before they can start the long, hard climb back to normality, I looked at the state I was in and accepted that the way I was playing the game of life was always going to put me on the losing side, no matter how hard I played. Instead of retreating into an alcoholic fog I had to turn and stare my demons right in the face and learn to accept them and live with them. Let nobody tell you that this is an easy road to travel, but at least it's a road that leads somewhere, whereas the road I'd taken with my incessant drinking was leading me nowhere but downwards.

Apart from my spell in Stanhope Street I have been

going to Alcoholics Anonymous meetings since the beginning, and I still attend on average twice a week. I've done general therapy, two years of primal therapy, six months on the inner child and two years rebirthing. I went to Aiseiri for a month and have attended countless seminars and shorter courses. I've read numerous books and gained enormous benefit from prayer and meditation. Most of all I've worked on myself constantly, learning what's of value to me and what's not, and that spiritual development is not about getting but about dropping – about giving away your co-dependency rather than adding more baggage.

Victories are often small, but repeated small victories gives me renewed hope. Like, for example, the time when I was walking in the park with Glen and Jordana and a dreadful panic attack came upon me. I had to get back into the car straight away and go home to Fontenoy Street, where I was living at the time. I said to Glen, 'I haven't felt so bad for a long time. I'll have to get some Valium somehow or other.' I was going into a panic spasm about every three minutes, with spells of dizziness as well. Glen helped me to walk around to my local doctor's surgery. When we arrived I went to put my hand up to ring the bell, but out of nowhere came the thought of not going in, that maybe I could deal with this myself without the aid of Valium. I've no idea why that thought should have struck me just then, but something inside me made me decide to face the panic and deal with it head on.

With that decision I could almost immediately feel the tension and alarm falling away, and I turned to Glen and asked him to take me back home without going into the surgery. Before I'd even crossed the road, every single symptom of the attack had disappeared and I felt totally rejuvenated. I was even more elated by the realisation that I had managed to control the attack without recourse to pills.

I hadn't understood what had happened at the time, although I learned later that it was simply that I had decided to accept the pain and had stopped trying to blot it out with artificial aids. Fighting and resisting our feelings only makes them worse. When we surrender to them and tell ourselves it's okay to feel this way, the miracle happens. Interestingly, that was the last major panic attack I had.

I would not like to convey the sense that my recovery is permanent or that I don't suffer lapses like everybody else. Every day I live with my deepest, darkest emotions and maybe I'll have to live with them to the day I die. But I learned eventually, after much pain, that there just might be a winner in me.

The serious panic attacks more or less stopped after about six years of no drinking and much therapy, and I've been thankfully free of them since. Those attacks must have been nature's way, as with the eruption of a volcano, of releasing my repressed emotions. Something had to give and this was the way those emotions broke through. So I learned that by allowing myself to be in a state of fear twenty-four hours each day and by facing into that fear I would be less inclined to panic. That acceptance has really worked.

Of course some anxiety still comes on me if I feel betrayed, abandoned or rejected, and I may be destined to be plagued with these demons for the rest of my life. I feel the threat of those feelings all the time and all the feelings can be traced back to my experiences as a child. Yet I feel confident that if I keep facing into it I'll beat it some day and come to terms with all my early traumas.

Strangely, but perhaps understandably, the only times I can feel totally comfortable with those feelings occur when I'm not in a serious relationship with a woman. Then I feel I'm as healthy and as normal as the next guy, but when I make that commitment the fear instantly resurfaces.

Now that I've been receiving counselling for about twelve years to help me deal with the traumas from my early childhood, I've learned that it's not the memories of my early days that cause my problems so much as the unexpressed emotions from that period. Only in recent times have I been able to accept what happened in the past and understand that I can't change it. I've had therapy to help me with this particular part of the problem, which is the core issue for me. I've also been back to Daingean for the first time and I've let myself off the hook instead of blaming myself and giving myself such a hard time. I've given up the people-pleasing and

I've stopped most of my destructive behaviour patterns and negative modes of thought.

In searching for explanations and solutions I've studied the writings of many experts, including Deepak Chopra and especially the late Jesuit Anthony de Mello, who has become a sort of hero to me. I've read his book *Awareness* at least a dozen times and I'm likely to read it many more times. I've also studied him on video. He brings us truth, which is why he ran foul of the Church, and he gives me direction. He tells it like it is and gets you to own your own problems instead of palming them off on other people, and he tells you that you have to find the solution to your own problems.

As de Mello would say, an apple falls from a tree by itself, with no help from anybody, when it's ripe. So with awareness, many of our problems just fall away too, with no help from us. What you're aware of you're in control of, but what you're not aware of is in control of you.

I attended a seminar in Dublin last year; one of the speakers, John Bradshaw, who has been enormously successful with a television series called *Bradshaw on the Family* in the USA, reckoned that it usually takes between thirteen and fifteen years away from a major addiction of any kind before someone can hit on their core or primary issues, and that's certainly true in my case.

I've benefited enormously from Bradshaw's book *Homecoming*, which helps me heal my inner child as well as helping me, as an adult, take sole responsibility for myself, my feelings and my actions. To some extent it helps me, in effect, to become my own parent, a task that is severely hampered by the fact that as a child I had no role models. But I have to do it. Therapy has helped in this regard too, and I had to learn to be a parent to my own children.

I've heard the argument, although not from professional counsellors, that if I just spent my whole day keeping busy writing songs, reading, recording, performing, doing interviews or whatever, I would just forget about my woes and they would disappear. In reality, I believe that such a course of action would just reinforce my apparently natural tendency to escape from problems instead of facing up to them. In my case it would be an avoidance of the fear of betrayal, a fear which can be traced right back to my mother's behaviour all those years ago, but a fear which I have to face, not hide from.

In the course of being interviewed for this book I was asked whether I have actually been betrayed since that time with my mother or whether I just carry the lingering fear of it. For a while the question stumped me. Had anyone, other than my mother, betrayed me in a similar way? Thinking it over made me realise that, when it comes to relationships with women, before they even get the chance to betray me my fear of it happening manifests itself in such a destructive way that it drives them away.

So perhaps I behave in a certain way towards them because of my fear of betrayal. I'll be on permanent alert for any evidence, no matter how flimsy or far-fetched, which will allow me to convince myself that I'm about to be betrayed again. Naturally, no woman will stay around any man who thinks or behaves like that.

I have suffered betrayal in other spheres of my life, but I don't think those instances relate to the deep-rooted fear I live with every day. For instance, I've dealt with some people in the music industry who betrayed me but I think that's a different type of betrayal. Most of those people are merely parasites who do not have sufficient ability or intelligence to make a living other than by leeching off musicians who trust them. But I can't see those sources of betrayal as having the same devastating effect as the mother who brought you into the world.

Even in recent years my fear of serious personal betrayal, no matter how unjustified, can spark off a feeling of deep anxiety that can last up to a year. Although I nearly always know in my head that there's no real basis for my suspicions, that knowledge doesn't help allay the fear in my heart. The problem is not something that I can expect to disappear overnight, so I have to continue to deal with it as best I can, but I fully believe that the truth will set me free and that avoiding the truth ultimately gets you nowhere.

Contrary to suspicions some have expressed to me, I

have never once seriously or consciously contemplated suicide. Either I'm too stubborn or I've always had an unshakeable inner conviction that I can somehow defeat this thing, that there really is a winner in me, as there is in all of us. I've always wanted to fight back rather than give in, and thankfully I've never completely lost that will to fight.

I believe that my determination comes from the Holy Spirit, and despite the best, and worst, efforts of the prisons and the reform schools, nobody has never broken that spirit in me. That indomitable spirit has been acknowledged by many, including Professor of Psychology Patricia Casey, to whom I recently went for an assessment, and it may explain why, in spite of everything I went through, I'm still here today, stronger than ever. A guy recently described himself as 'a very strong person who thinks he's weak', and maybe that was me for much of my life.

Every night I write down an inventory of that day, noting anybody I might have hurt and resolving to apologise to them. It's like going to confession to myself and it keeps me clear and stops guilt building up. As de Mello says, 'Hug your demons or they'll bite you in the ass!'

And there are highlights in my life. One of the most exciting things happened to me in my late forties something I had craved all my life – when I got my tonsils out! Yes, you can laugh if you like, but you have no idea what that meant to me. I remember when Dr

Collins, brother of my late friend Michael, gave me the news that it had to be done I went home as elated as I'd been for a long time. I drove through Blackrock with the windows of my car wound down, giving the thumbs up to bewildered strangers. The song 'Let Your Love Flow' by the Bellamy Brothers came on the radio and I sang along with it at the top of my voice through the busy streets of Dublin.

You are entitled to wonder why a man in his forties would react in this bizarre way to such a relatively mundane event, the sort of thing five-year-olds take in their stride. The operation was, after all, a necessary one, as my voice was becoming affected by years of incorrect vocal habits and decades of cigarette-smoking. But, like everything else, the reason for my joy went back to my childhood. Where I grew up there were two types of kids who were the envy of all the other kids, those who got their tonsils out and those who got their appendix out. A big fuss would be made over them. They'd get cards, sweets, comics, toys and loads of visitors to see them in the hospital. They'd have time off school, and they'd have no chores to do until they were fully recovered. But I'd been deprived of such privileges until now!

My hospitalisation occurred while I was undergoing an inner-child course with Louise McDonald and she played along with my enjoyment by bringing a red football to me as a present. It was one of the happiest moments in my adult life, but I don't really expect too many people to understand!

So sometimes we get our moments of deepest gratification from the most unlikely situations. While many would expect that my most memorable musical moments would be those with big crowds and standing ovations, that's not always the case. One of my most cherished recollections is of playing harmonica at the funeral of my friend Michael Collins, the guy who brought me news from the USA of Bono's well-documented statement about me. I'd known Michael since my teens, when he had been one of the volunteers – we used to call them 'Docs' – who helped out at the Belvedere Youth Club in Dublin's inner city. I used to go there on Friday evenings, and Michael was particularly helpful to me, trying to encourage me with my singing, giving me advice and boosting my confidence.

The two of us hung around with Richard Uzell and other mates like John Meehan and Robert Gallagher, and for a while he was the big brother I'd never had. He could have his breakfast with a tramp and his dinner with the President and treat them both the same. When I was arrested by the police once for not paying a fine, Michael came around to Mountjoy, paid the fine out of his own pocket and got me released. He later moved to California and became extremely wealthy, but we kept in touch.

The manner in which I heard of his death still shocks me to this day. I went in to meet a business colleague who gruffly said to me, with no preamble, 'Have you a friend called Michael Collins?' When I said I had, he callously said, 'Well he's dead', almost as if he was pleased to the bearer of such shocking news. I'll always cherish the memories of the fine, decent person that was Michael Collins.

I have an active social life, not least with my siblings. Despite, or perhaps because of, our deprived upbringing, I have a very good relationship with all of my sisters and my brother Pat, who has built up a fine photography business in Dublin. We all meet regularly and I still feel very protective towards all of them.

One thing concerns me considerably in regard to my recovery, some of which has been well documented in the media, and that's my 'celebrity' status. I realise that on the positive side it may help for others to know that somebody they regard as being as successful and as well-known as Don Baker could suffer like them and reach the depths of despair and then recover with some semblance of self-worth. That's the good part of it.

But although I push myself fairly hard towards spiritual growth, I'm the first to admit that I'm as likely to lapse as anybody else, and it can often be a case of three steps forward, two steps back. I have to admit that I've had a few drinks now and then, perhaps to test myself or to experiment. That might be risky, but I was able to stop when I wanted to. But I'm not going to beat myself up over it any more. I have no difficulty avoiding the occasions when drink is available and I've passed up countless invitations to drink as much as I wanted free of charge.

Doing more solo gigs and working in films has given me a greater sense of confidence anyway, but it scares me that some people might expect too much from me and see me as a kind of role model. It's not quite as simple as saying that, if I could recover, anyone can do it. I could slide backwards at any time.

It's something each individual has to tackle alone and it will require enormous courage and determination. The only way to heal pain is to feel it. You can't heal what you can't feel. Maybe some can't deal with that, and some have difficulty accepting that their recovery may have to be on a truly spiritual basis.

Of course I'm delighted to help anybody I can who has suffered in any similar way to me, and people come up to me regularly after gigs telling how I've either inspired them or inspired someone they know. After I appeared in the television documentary *States of Fear*, about the brutal treatment of young people in Irish institutions, I received many letters, including some from politicians and doctors, praising my courage for speaking out and referring to me as an inspiration to others, but those responses actually scare me a little. I've often suspected that I have the power to heal others, but that too scares me. I don't want to be a practising healer. I'm a musician, so maybe I can channel those beneficial energies into my performances instead.

I shun the path of the healer because I don't want to be set up like that, risking a fall and then bringing down with me anyone else who might be clinging to me for support. Interfering in others' lives can be dangerous, even when we think we're doing it for the best, so I won't take somebody else's responsibility away from them or accept any position on someone else's pedestal.

Yes, I've committed crimes and hurt people in many ways over the years, but I've been hurt too, and I'm satisfied in my heart that I've paid the price. In some respects I've paid a price considerably out of proportion to my actual wrongdoing.

It's taken me fifteen hard and painful years to get to where I am now. I still have much to work through, especially in relation to my mother. I get a little scared when I realise that I don't have any ambitions to achieve or challenges to accept, other than the healing of my life and the desire to be at peace. But then, maybe those goals are more than enough for anybody.

Nor can I ever see myself settling anywhere else but in Dublin. I've travelled a lot overseas but I always feel safest and most comfortable back home. Even the mention of the word 'passport' sometimes makes me uneasy. I spent some time living with a lawyer in Los Angeles, but I found the people so plastic and so pretentious that I never took to the place and returned to the comfort of familiar Dublin.

I've a successful career and five children whom I love. I believe I've become a very good, responsible, reliable and caring parent, and maybe some day I'd like a normal family life with a comfortable relationship and a few kids around me. I know I've still got a long way to go before I achieve any level of emotional stability, but I'd like to think I've finally proved to myself that there's a winner in me.

I hope you find the winner in you too.